WH

STANDS

STILL

WITH A COMPREHENSIVE STUDY GUIDE

By Rebecca Hickson

To Marg,

I hope you enjoy these writings

Rebecca

WHEN TIME

STANDS

STILL

CONTENTS

ACKNOWLEDGMENTS

People go through their personal journey. We travel many miles through rugged mountainous terrain, a desert here, and an oasis there. In our pilgrimage we all have a hope of affecting people's lives in a meaningful way. To leave a legacy to those we come to know and love. I have compiled this book of true stories of many people, who have made a difference in my life. For those who have gone before me, I dedicate this book: To Sue, Larry, Tony, Ronnie, Tommy, Sandy, Robbie, Steve, Marg and Karyn: Their shortened lives left a seed within my heart, marking the days in my life, when time stood still. In the stillness, came growth, endurance, strength and a closer walk with Jesus Christ my Lord. May this book be a living legacy for all who have influenced my life in a special way.

To those who helped me edit and reedit, thank you for your inspiration, suggestions and constructive criticism. You helped make these journal writings a readable book. Thank you to my editor Shannon Hazell. Thanks to the late Harold Ross who is now gone to be with the Lord. Wherever you are Donna, thank you for toning my skills in creative writing class.

To my wonderful husband and best friend Don, thank you for your love, support, and encouragement and for believing in me, especially during the times, I didn't believe in myself. I appreciate your steadfast loyalty and support.

You have my eternal love.

To my children, Kyle and Maegan, thank you for your patience, support and words of wisdom. Thank you, for making me laugh, when I felt like crying and for loving me through all my ups and downs. I have learned so much from you. You are precious.

To my friends, thank you for standing by me through trials and tribulations. For listening to me whine and being patient with me through the healing process. You have a special place in my heart. You are God's gift to me.

To staff at Xulon Press, thank you for helping me to become a published author. Thanks for work done and for your help and support.

To you the reader: When time stands still, may you find the hope, endurance, and strength, from the Lord Jesus Christ. For He gets all the glory, honour and praise forever and ever. Amen!

INTRODUCTION

This book began in a grade twelve adult learning class in 1997. At this time, I was a stay at home mom and had been involved in church activities. This was a time to stretch my legs and go back out into the real world. I would leave my nice safe group of Christian friends, bible studies and prayer groups to go down a different road.

God began to increase my passion for writing. This challenge would become a growing experience in my relationship with Jesus. Little did I know at the time, God would use my journal writings to bring healing and give me some new perspective about life? From my daily journals, God would put together a collage of testimonies. He inspired me to make this book for others who struggle with similar trials or experiences. Please allow me to take you back to my childhood and family roots.

It was a day When Time Stood Still. Well, not exactly. I imagine my lungs gasped to take that first breath. In the year of 1961, I was born into a family of six children. We lived in a small lake town in Keswick, Ontario. My parents owned Windsor's Boats & Cabins, which was a summer resort.

I was raised in a country setting at a time when Lake Simcoe was a quiet, picturesque lake. The lake had a character all of its own. In the winter we couldn't wait for the first freeze-over, so we could skate or play hockey in the fresh cool air. I remember shooting the hockey puck and chasing it for what seemed miles. Then we would come in for a nice hot roast beef dinner.

Every Spring we watched the ice in the bay melt. We would watch the last huge iceberg come down the bay. Like a bulldozer the dark grey monster slowly made its way, leaving carnage of broken docks along its path. Many years, I watched my Mum's tear-filled eyes as she hoped and prayed our docks would not be taken out. The extra expense and work of rebuilding the docks every Spring brought an extra burden. But we would rebuild and be ready for the opening day of pike season on the May 24th long weekend. Some years, the rain would fall or the winds would blow and the long anticipated opening weekend would be a disappointing one. My Mum would count the change that would bring the next week's groceries. Being a small boat and cabin resort, we depended on the weather.

The Fall season would bring duck hunters. My brothers would prepare for the hunt by making decoys and cedar duck-hides. The cool frost would lie upon the water's edge. The quacking of the hunters' duck calls would ring in the air early in the morning. Gunshots were fired and pellets would fall from the sky like rain.

The seasons would come and go along with the years. Today the place is gone and there is no trace of my childhood, or the hard work and long days my parents put in. It was another lifetime ago, it seems. The cabins have been torn down and replaced with a house. The boats no longer sit in their stalls at the docks. Most of the people who stayed there are long gone too. Weeds now fill the lake, where we once swam in the fresh water. We take our memories and flip through the picture books remembering when . . . Some memories we may wish to forget, but others are treasured.

I remember my Mum always had a load of laundry on the line. They were the whitest bed sheets. Customers used to tease Mum saying she should make a Tide commercial.

Those bed sheets seemed to blend nicely with the country air and the sweet essence of the lake. However, I will always remember my Mum for more than her laundry. I told her the other day that when I grow up, I want to be just like her. I'm in my forties now, but I will always be her little girl. She is a model of strength, faith, encouragement and Motherly love. There is a lasting bond that took place the day my Mum gave birth to me. I appreciate so much the wisdom she shares with me from living eighty years of life.

Everyone has a story to tell. I would like to share with you some of my personal stories. Childhood brings many wonderful memories along with the sad. It seems each memory becomes a little more precious as time goes by. I would like to take a reminiscent gander back to those days and invite you to come along for the journey.

Operating a summer resort, we ran a small snack bar that sold candy, chocolate bars, fast foods and fishing bait. The summers were very busy. The first fisherman would be knocking at our door at 5:30 in the morning. The last customer would come in as the big red floodlight shined out across the bay into the dark of night. After the last customer left for the day, we would all race up to the house covering our heads so the bats wouldn't land in our hair.

Having cabins filled with new customers every weekend, we met many different types of people. Some stayed and made it a permanent cottage every summer. Uncle Ernie was one of our annual customers. He was everyone's uncle. Every summer for thirty years he occupied cabin number five.

Uncle Ernie loved to sell candies at the snack bar to the little children. He would joke with us and give us candies when my Mum and Dad were not looking. I remember this shiny nickel that he nailed to the snack bar floor. I could never figure out why, but I couldn't pick that nickel up. I knew it would buy a lot of bubble gum, if I could just get it up off that floor. So, I spent many hours determinately trying to pick up that nickel. I never did succeed. Perhaps it was the first lesson in perseverance of many lessons to come? Uncle Ernie had quite a sense of humour. He got such a kick out of watching every customer who bent down to pick up that nickel. You could say Uncle Ernie was my parent's right-hand man.

One night as a storm began to blow into the shore, the waves of the rough water came up over the docks. The aluminium boats pounded against the wooden slots. Many times the storms would blow in quickly leaving little time to tie the boats up firmly. One particular day, as everyone was working fervently to get all the boats in place, no one noticed that I was standing on the dock. I was about three years old and light as a feather. One of the waves swept over me like a giant hand knocking me into the water. I believe it was my heavenly Father's protective hand, which gave me the ability to grab onto the side of the dock. In the frenzy of tying up the boats, Uncle Ernie noticed these tiny little fingers hanging desperately onto the edge of the dock. With my head fully emerged under the water, little fear-filled eyes stared up at him. He reached down, grabbed my hair and pulled me out from the water, saving my life.

One could say that I grew up surrounded by good fishermen. Heard every fish story ever told. I also love to fish. As a child I spent a lot of time catching and cleaning fish. There was always a BBQ cooking at one of the cabins. If I couldn't catch any fish, I'd net a sucker from the minnow tank, clean it, then cook it on one of the customers BBQ's.

Most good fishermen always take great pride and joy in their catch. I learned all about the bait you could use. I owned my own worm business at the age of twelve. Every week my Dad went catching minnows. Sometimes I would tag along to observe and learn. Each of my siblings took a turn catching minnows with Dad. Now I wonder, if these experiences were all part of the preparation for the day, when I would become a fisher of men? There is a purpose in all things.

There are endless stories I could tell. We went through many years together with many people. Our lives were intertwined together. Some customers became life long friends. Others came and went just as quick as they came. Some touched our hearts in a special way. We shared in their triumphs and in their heartaches. Many lives somehow left a picture in our memories.

A couple of customers stand out in my memory. Andy was a quiet man with no family. He was a trucker, who came up every weekend and went fishing all day. Andy always wore his silver hard hat that had his name written on the front. He would grab a coke and a Sweet Marie chocolate bar before he headed back to the big city. Andy was killed in an accident when his tractor-trailer Jack-knifed. Andy's life was like a page taken from the book of our lives. Perhaps Andy is still fishing? Maybe he went to fish in a heavenly bay?

We had another customer with the name Ernie. We called him Little Ernie. Every weekend, he would bring his wife Marge, their four daughters and their little dog to our place. Little Ernie would go fishing and his girls would picnic and swim at the lake. Our home was home to anyone who came to vacation or just get away for the day. They loved coming up to our place so much that when little Ernie died of cancer, they wanted us to have his memorial service by the lake. There they laid his ashes in the rippling waters of Cooks Bay.

Within our memories we store many treasures to remember. We have the privilege to share much laughter and good times with all those people who pass through our lives. This book is just one picture after another, which tell my homegrown story. We all have a story to tell.

Step into my journal and begin a walk down memory lane. Share in my joys and my sorrows. In doing so, you could be my friend and I could be yours. I hope my journal book also brings you whatever it is God wants to relate to your life. It is my prayer that this book will help you find hope, strength and love to help you to be an over-comer in the days of your life, "When Time Stands Still.

1

Breaking Silence
Letter to a friend

Pain of the past but hope for tomorrow

My dear friend:

I'm writing you today understanding the grief you bear. I send my love and sympathy to you. The loss of your loved one has me reflecting back on many childhood memories, old photos, which I have stored for quite some time, in the corner of my mind. I would like to share with you video footage unravelled from within, which helped me to remember when I was ten, and my friend Lou-Ann was eleven years old. Tony, a young boy, who also was ten years old, came to my mind. I did not know him well. I just knew him in passing.

My friend Lou-Ann knew him. In fact, she had a crush on him. I will never forget the day I heard the news. It was a hot summer day. I was sitting on the dock basking in the sun, totally enjoying my summer vacation. My friend came walking down the long, shaky dock. The dock was not the only thing shaking. Lou-Ann's whole foundation was shaken that day. I could see the tears stream down her face. Her brown eyes were hidden from the redness of swollen eyelids.

Her naturally freckled face and life filled smile, were transformed into a blank, troublesome expression. She was overwhelmed with questions and grief. Between heartfelt sobs, she blurted out, "Tony . . . and his friend were killed today . . . Hit . . . by a car . . . while riding double on his bike." She was very upset, and crying. I tried to console her, not really understanding the loss she felt.

I wonder if anyone gave her feelings any consideration? We never talked about Tony again after that day. Lou-Ann and her family moved away a few months later. After all the time that has elapsed, I wonder if Lou-Ann still thinks about Tony? Years later I had my first crush on a boy. His name was Ronnie, our paperboy. Ronnie, a few boys in the neighbourhood and I, went to school together. After school, we played sports, hide and seek . . . I can still smell that cool fresh air and hear the clacking of our hockey sticks hitting the puck. I was like one of the boys. We fought for that little black puck like it was worth gold. He shoots. She scores. We always won the game when we were on the same side. There was something different about Ronnie. For some strange reason, my hands would sweat and my heart would skip a beat whenever Ronnie was near. I remember trying to teach him how to play the guitar. As I placed his sweaty nail bitten fingers on the guitar strings, I noticed he was nervous too. He was my secret admirer who put a little love note and a bubble gum ring in with our daily newspaper. Who else could it have been? And they called it Puppy L o v e . . . Oh I guess we will never know . . . He looked so cute in his karate outfit eating those Dads cookies as he so boyishly dipped them into his cold milk. Our parents were friends. In a small lake town, everybody knows everybody.

I'll never forget the time when we were playing Nicky nine doors. It was a cool Fall night and the sky was dark as midnight with dampness hanging in the air. We sneakily knocked on this little painted door. The paint was peeling like a banana. Most of the houses were old cottages that really needed some refurbishing. The yards were messy and every yard had a clothing line. That night we knocked on the door then ran like the wind. Ronnie was running full tilt, and I was not going to be left behind. Running with such speed we did not see the clothesline, which hung about neck level. Up went our feet and down went our backsides. The landing was cushioned nicely by some rather soft stinky smelling dog poo. Barely breathing, our hands holding our throats, we managed to get back on our feet and keep running. Fear motivated of course. Ronnie was really hurt. Embarrassed and in pain, he was trying not to cry. We were both covered in dog poo. He tried to hide his pain by getting angry at our unsympathetic friends, who laughed hysterically at our circumstance.

My friend, do you remember the day we were up at Larue's farm with Ronnie and Johnny. They proudly showed us their gas bombs. Johnny accidentally caught his leg on fire when some gasoline spilled onto his pant leg. We frantically rolled him around the dirt like a rag doll until we put out the flames. We carried him back to his house and tried to help him. He didn't want to tell his Mother what happened, even though he was in horrible pain. Thinking we could help remedy his pain, we remembered that sunburn cream commercial. We thought if that soothing cream cooled sunburns, surely it would sooth Johnny's burned leg. I guess we shouldn't have thought so much. As it turned out, Johnny had third degree burns on his leg. Our naive treatment on his burn did more harm than good.

It did teach us a few things. Don't believe everything you see on TV and matches and gasoline doesn't mix.

I wrote my first song for Ronnie, he inspired me so. We went through high school getting on the bus at the local bus stop every day. Then Ronnie met Charlene and they pretty much stayed together all through high school. Thus, my crush ended.

Then there was Ronnie's best friend Sandy. He was such a tease, always embarrassing me. I think he liked to see my face turn red. He had a lot of nerve though. I remember at the Miami Beach picnic when Sandy and Ronnie dressed up like women and put on a comedy act. Their picture made the local newspaper.

The last time I saw them we were at an anniversary party. A few weeks later, their names made the local newspaper again. The headline news read: "**Two Local Men Killed in Motorcycle Collision.**" I received a phone call telling me Ronnie and Sandy were both killed, when they were riding home from a party. Ronnie's motorcycle hit a car sending them both landing in a cornfield. He only had his new motorcycle for a week.

I couldn't go to the funeral to pay my respects, as I was bedridden. I never had the chance to say goodbye. At the time, I was married and expecting my second child. We had a lot of fun times together, didn't we? I still can't believe they are gone; they were so young, the prime of life some would say.

Then there was Robbie? He had the cutest blonde locks of hair and blue eyes you have ever seen. Robbie chipped my front tooth when we were wrestling. He always came to our snack bar to buy candy. He was the only boy in his family with four sisters. His laugh echoed through the bus everyday.

I received the news a year later, after Ronnie and Sandy's death, that Robbie was also killed. He was on his way home to his newlywed wife. They were expecting their first child. He was stopped on his motorcycle at a stop sign, when a car smashed into him. He never had a chance. Again, I was so dismayed and in disbelief.

You probably never met Tommy. He was like my little brother. We played Mod Squad and I would gag him with my socks. Tommy and his brother Billy and I built so many forts together. I always had a protective spirit when it came to Tommy. As children, we always stuck together like a mini gang. We used to pretend we were daredevils, to the extreme sometimes. Driving our bicycles off the dock. We would see who could climb the highest or who could spit the farthest. We had a little band. We would spend hours in the boathouse practising for our annual corn roast. Tommy was our little drummer boy. Somehow time stood still and we all grew into adults. Our lives all took different paths. Our little fantasy world where the good guys win and I come to the rescue came to an end.

If I could make time stand still, I would be at the intersection of their lives and warn them. Slow down Ronnie. Watch out Robbie, a car is coming. I would stand on that bridge with Tommy like when we were kids. And I would tell him he has a friend, that we need a drummer boy in our lives. I'd tell him I love him and that he is special to all of us. I'd tell him not to jump. That is if he did jump? We never did find out what really happened to Tommy, whether he jumped or was pushed? God knows.

Instead, we all walk in times of stillness. We are moulded by our experiences for some great purpose. Our questions wait for answers that we couldn't possibly understand. Maybe we don't really need to know the answers. I had to say my goodbyes to these friends who were all a big part of my childhood, thanking God that I got to know each one of them.

My friend, as you can see, I believe I relate in a small way to the loss you are feeling. I too have felt that loss with each of these friends. All of them died in their early twenties. Time ticked away life's precious moments, and one by one I would feel that same loss Lou-Ann also felt years earlier. The poem "Breaking Silence" represents the memories I have of Ronnie, Sandy, Robbie and Tommy. Their deaths were not pretty, snuffed out . . . I would rather remember their lives, not their deaths. Still, I always look past the funerals to eternity. Will I see them again? God is the judge. Ironically, death is a part of life, a reminder of our own immortality. The death of your loved can be overwhelmingly difficult to bear. God's loving Spirit has given me strength and comfort in moments of grief. I pray He gives you comfort also. The Bible has shown me God's love. The age-old questions often arise at funerals. How could God take away my child? How could he let this happen? Why? . . . The questions can become endless. In our grief no answer would be good enough. Deep within my heart I know God cares and loves each of us. He loves us so much He allowed His own Son to hang six hours on the cross. He loves us enough to allow his Son to suffer, nails through hands and feet, ridiculed and beaten into unbearable pain. He allowed His precious Son to die to save us from death. Why did God go to such drastic measures with the example of His Son Jesus Christ? Possibly as one way of showing us that we have a God who does understand and feel our pain.

It is so hard to comprehend the depth of God's love or the concept He used to demonstrate His love, but it is true. Death has a way of bringing people closer together. It tears down the man-made walls of toughness and pride, bringing out the vulnerability in people. We could also call it humanity. Whatever we call it, it does not have to take death to tear down the walls. I have comfort in knowing Christ conquered death. Let us strive to conquer life. Love each other, the way God intended us to love each other, from the very beginning. The way God loves us, yesterday, today, and tomorrow with unfailing love. Let us follow his example.

I don't believe it is always possible for us to find out what God's purposes are in our lives. It is important that we learn to accept the hand we are dealt. Learn and be strengthened, so we can help others. In drawing closer to God then we can begin to understand who God is to each one of us. As we learn to trust and rely on God, He will put together the missing pieces of the puzzle of our individual lives. Our lives become so intertwined in the lives of others. There are so many other people out there like you and I, who also need help with their grief. It is ironic, but sometimes one person's loss might be another person's gain. In the early grieving stages, we don't want to hear these kinds of words, which are meant for comfort. However, there is time to grasp these truths.

May God's understanding and compassion grow in each of us. May we learn to fully rely on Him for everything. May God be with you my friend. May you truly find comfort, peace and that blessed assurance of the Lord. May He ease your pain and help you to grieve the loss of your loved one.

In memory of:
Tony - 1971
Ronnie Elcomb, Sandy Turcott - 1985
Robbie Brown - 1986
Tommy Lemay - 1990

Breaking Silence

We played and danced like leaves in the wind.
Breaking silence with our laughter.
Wrestling in the grassy field,
    like wild flowers amongst growing wheat.

A path we trod each day to our special forest glade.
To build together our secret little fort.
Camouflaged with cedar foliage,
    surrounded by tall evergreens of sorts.

The bond of childhood friends blended harmoniously
with nature's freshness.
Newfangled ideas each day,
    busy having fun.

Planting memories, with each game,
every spoken word.
Watering seeds of love like a misty rain,
    advances life.

It seems like another lifetime ago.
Weeds grow amongst a rose bush.
Thorns and thistles choke the worn path,
    with the change time did bring.

Today, I watch my children.
Freedom of expression embellishes their faces.
Running free, with gleaming smiles,
lighting up a cloudy day.
    Yet, a reminder of yesterday . . .

Cement cemeteries replace the wonder of old trees.
The seeds of memories remain.
Friends are gone, but not forgotten,
    rooted deeply are the watered seeds.

Bodies sealed within cold coffins.
Others trapped by man-made walls, quenching friendships.
Like polluting smoke stacks, and noisy cars
    suffocate the air of a dying earth.

Stop the hands on the clock,
which tick away life's precious moments.
Release the seed of hope and love.
Set free the child trapped within, to dance again,
    like leaves in the wind.

Breaking Silence
CHAPTER 1

Job 2:13 "Then they sat on the ground with him for seven days and seven nights. No one said a word to him, because they saw how great his suffering was."

The book of Job gives page after page of examples of what not to say. Their well-intended advice and accusations gradually change to assumptions, false accusations and misinterpretation of Job and God's motives. Job's three friends compassionate silence was more help to Job, then all their misplaced advice or comments.

1. In counselling or giving advice to a hurting person, what does the Bible book of Job instruct us to say and not to say? Refer to the book of Job and His three friends' Bildad, Zophar and Eliphaz.

2. What was God's response to Job's friends about their advice? What else does the Bible tell us about death, which will give comfort to a grieving person?

3. In your own words, how would you describe the death of Jesus? Explain the process He went through and why? See Matthew 27:45-56, Luke 23:44-49 and Isaiah 53:12.

4. What can we learn about God and the depth of His love for us, from reading the following scripture reference: 1 Peter 2:24 "He himself bore our sins in his body on the tree, so that we might die to sins and live for righteousness; by his wounds you have been healed."

For further study read Psalm 71:20-21 "Though you have made me see troubles, many and bitter, you will restore my life again, from the depths of the earth. You will increase my honour and comfort me once again." In stressful times we can find comfort in the hope promised throughout the Bible.

5. What do the following verses say about friendship? 1 Samuel 31, Proverbs 18:24, 27:6, Ecclesiastes 4:10-12 Samuel 20.

2

Time Warp

Defeating the monster called time warp

I just pinched myself and I didn't feel much of anything. I am still numb from the impact, shock, or whatever they call it. It does not really matter. What was it all about? I'm not sure, a brush with death - staring death right in the face? Was I ripped from the clutches of death or the clutches of life? Enough with the barrage of questions. Let us take a car ride I will never forget.

I started the car and brushed the snow from the windows. Slowly, like candy floss melting into syrup, big fluffy snowflakes dropped to the ground. In a hurry again, I allowed no time to admire the beautiful snowflakes. No time was taken to collect my thoughts or take a breath of fresh air. I found myself caught in that "time warp" of life's fast moving lane. It is a "time warp" that so many of us get pulled into. Just when we think we have a few extra minutes to get to that next appointment, the monster called "time warp" causes us to be late. I left school fifteen minutes early. I should have taken that extra time to slow the pace. Guess what? I didn't. You see, that fifteen minutes extra really meant, I had another thing I could get done before picking my children up from school.

Rushed for time, I followed the flow of traffic onto the highway, the same way I do every day, on the drive home. The cars raced by me, spraying slush into the air. The cars wheels heated the ice, like a zamboni on a hockey rink. A chemical reaction of cold air, water, and snow mixed with a greasy black road, started a chain wreck reaction. Panicking drivers in the cars ahead of me hit their brakes. I felt numb as I watched the cars in front of me pile into each other, metal . . . upon metal . . . upon metal . . .

Time as I knew it changed into a time suspension, forcing me to make a decision that could affect many lives. I was closing in fast on a wall of crumbled cars and bright red taillights. "Hit the breaks gently," I said to myself, still trying to remain calm. The car started to slide. "I am still going too fast. If I don't do something soon, I'm going to pile into the back of them too." With no option left, I hit the breaks hard. The car began to slide in the direction of the guardrail. Quickly I turned the wheel to avoid smashing into it. The car spun around intractably, yet the car was in God's control. I took my foot off the brakes, bracing myself for what would happen next. White knuckles gripped the steering wheel. The car turned in slow motion. There before me, and getting closer, was a very hard looking cement median, with which I was soon to make contact.

For the next thirty seconds time stood still. No longer did I have control over my destiny, yet peace came over me. I remember feeling a bit like a child on a roller coaster ride, having faith that the ride would end safely. Despite all the screams, we have an acceptance of the outcome. The ride will end and we will have gotten our money's worth.

Wham! Snap! Crunch! That was some ride. Wow. I am still alive. Nothing is broken. Wait a minute. Ah . . . Ah . . . Ah . . . What is that coming at me?

Looking out my front window I see a forty-ton tractor-trailer sliding down the road toward me. Just when I thought the ride was over, they sent me around again. Dying is one thing. I can accept death, knowing I have eternal life through my Saviour Jesus Christ. The thought of that big monster of a truck crushing me like a bug did not appeal to me at all. Hyperventilating, gasping for air, my breathing became sporadic. I had to try to get out of there. In a state of panic I tried to decide, whether to get out and run or try to drive the crumpled car away on the slippery ice. Forgetting how to drive, I began shifting the automatic stick shift, like a monkey in a car for the first time. Swallowing the lump in my throat, I watched the transport truck slide to a stop, feet in front of me.

"Thank you Lord." "Praise Jesus." I thought, as I went on to drive the broken little car off the deathly icy road. For the next three hours I sat in the car, thinking about what did and did not happen, contemplating God's power, his love, and his grace.

I learned some important lessons that day: Listen to God when He tells me to be still and listen to his voice. For many weeks God had been telling me to slow my pace. I think He meant it. Second, No one has control over life or death except the one who created it. "God!" The end of life as we know it can come in a flash. I have learned to appreciate everyone and everything. Each of these are important parts of our pilgrimage here. Before God flashes that big red light for the final time, give that extra second, that extra minute. Try not to let the "time warps" of life tick away life's precious moments. You do not know when the clock will stop. Warning . . . Watch out for that "time warp."

Time Warp

The rushing wind blows into town.
The town people run for cover.
They fear the unexpected.
Hide from what they cannot see.
It must be a storm, a raging twister.
Must run! Run! Hide from it Mister.
They pack up their clothes.
Load up their cars.
Gather old photos of memories, scars.
They are all running. They don't know where.
They are creating chaos, mass confusion.
Leaving a path of senseless destruction.
They hurry and hurry, racing for time.
Rushing so fast to erase humankind.
Never to take a moment to embrace,
The quiet stillness of peaceful grace.
In their haste and self-preservation,
They themselves destroy the nation.
Hiding from the unexpected,
That which they cannot see.
Twas not a raging twister.
Should have stayed a moment longer Mister.
The raging wind was a warm Chinook.
Should have taken that moment to look,
To enjoy the quiet, stillness and grace,
But instead in haste,
They missed out on God's Grace.
That peaceful warmth of His embrace.

Time Warp
CHAPTER 2

In Genesis chapter 1, we see an example of taking time. God takes six days to create the heavens, earth, day and night, land and sky, sun and moon, animals and man. He didn't just go poof, although God could have created it all at once. God took each task one day at a time until He completed His work. Then He took a day to rest.

1. Why did God take six days to create everything? Why not make it all instantaneously?

2. In this fast moving age we live in, it is very easy to get caught in that "Time Warp." What should be our priority in life, when we line up with God's Word? Reference: Ephesians 5:15, Colossians 4:5, Psalm 37:7, 46:10, Zechariah 2:13.

3. For further study read the Book of Haggai.

4. Sometimes, when we are caught up in busyness, we lose track of our priorities. What was God saying through the prophet Haggai to the people when He said, "Give careful thought to your ways?" (Haggai chapter 1)

5. What made the temple so important? (Haggai chapter 2) What did the temple symbolize? How does this book of the Bible relate to your relationship with God today?

6. What encouragement, warning, and hope did God offer Israel? What does God offer you by building your house for the Lord? For more historical information, read Ezra 1-6 and Ezra 5:1-2.

There is often consequence to ignoring God. An example "Be still and listen." A famous song "I did it my way" is a very common scenario, sometimes with horrific results. In our quest to get things done fast, our way instead of God's way, we can exclude and hurt others around us in the process, especially God.

3

The Bandage

❧

Healing old wounds

Do you have a lifetime of shut-up words bottled within you? Does it seem like no matter how far you try to push them down, they poke their ugly heads out of that glass bottle and say, "I'm back?" Maybe it is a wound that caused much pain and you have never verbalized your hurt. Instead a no-name bandage has covered up the wound. It is a wound that you have never treated with proper care, but left untreated for many years. Today the wound is deeper then ever and still covered by that same old bandage. In your heart you believe it is going to hurt when you pull off that old bandage. Then again you may find it will heal quickly. Dare to take off that bandage?

The heavenly Father can help heal wounds. One day He ripped the bandage from one of my old wounds. When He did a lifetime of shut-up words, and bottled emotions poured out like a pure drink offering.

It was not my typical Sunday. I was not in church. However, God still enveloped me in His love and embraced us with His awesomeness. The children and I buckled into the car as we prepared for the long drive to my parents. A grey cloud was covering the earth, like a heavy wool blanket. The blanket had a small tear in it, where we could see fragments of light blue peaking through the clouds.

Looking through the windows of the car gave us a feeling of peace and a wonder of the beauty our eyes beheld. We were driving through God's glass boutique. Crystals of ice glazed the trees, while a gentle east wind blew. Delicate fragments of ice dispersed through the air. Warmth arose as the sun slowly peeked through the grey clouds melting the glassy ice. Large pieces of ice fell sporadically from the stiff branches, shattering into pearls of water. My mind took panoramic pictures as I looked across the horizon, stretching my vision to the limit. The beauty of the view captured my heart. It was so spectacular.

The closeness with God, witnessing His awesome creation, allowed my children and me to have quality conversation. Perhaps it was a time to admire the beauty God surrounds us with, or a time to tame our hearts for the contrast we were soon to witness.

We arrived at the hospital to take my Dad home for the day. My eyes were not prepared for the transition I would see, but perhaps my heart was. It had been a month since I last saw my Dad. Physically he had deteriorated, more than I had imagined. They had given him new medication that made him lethargic. He seemed so weak and feeble. I became overwhelmed with sympathy for him and all the other patients at the hospital. Many patients seemed lifeless and alone, sitting in the stench of their dirty diapers. The treatment of the elderly people did not seem humane. The corrosive smell of stale urine made me gag. Humbling? Yes! Unknown to me, hidden within the midst of this horrific sight, God was removing a bandage. I found myself feeling great love for my father, which I never allowed myself to feel. The time was short, but each moment precious and well spent. We took my Dad home for the day. I did and said things that day that I would never have imagined. It was like a day taken from a page in a fairy tale.

I spent time talking to Dad while washing his face and cutting his hair. It was more than works of the day; it was the unspoken emotional bond that took place for the first time in my life. It was a bond between father and child. When God removed that bandage, my wounds began to heal. He tore down a wall. I saw into my father's heart. Though he said not a word, I knew he was happy and content to be at home with Mum and I. His smile said it all.

My Dad ended up going into a convalescence home, where he lived out the rest of his days. On thanksgiving 2000, my Dad passed away. It was another eye opener. One of those phone calls which sent me to my Dad's bedside. Once again the river of my emotions came flowing forth as if God had opened up a dam. As part of the healing process of our hurts, sometimes we are dipped into that quickly flowing river to look at the debris of the past. That phone call and the time I had to reflect while driving to the home, forced me to look again, but this time I looked a little deeper. I find God works His wonders in us, a little bit at a time.

In my narrow interpretation of my life and the role my Dad played, I had always looked at the negative rather than the positive. It is ironic that when we are close to losing a loved one, sometimes we gain a new perspective. Hidden in the silent river for so many years was the unspoken love. I wonder why I have spent so many years blaming my Dad, only seeing the negative? Was it possibly easier to put the blame on him for all my shortcomings? That way I never had to take the responsibility for my choices of action. It was easier to blame my Dad.

When I arrived at the home to see my Dad that day, my heart melted at the sight of this frail little man. I cry still at his passing. Remembering now, there were so many good things. His love may not have been shown according to any book. Maybe he wasn't like the Dad on that old television show, 'Father Knows Best'.

My Dad loved the only way he knew how to love. His love was expressed in his strong hard working hands, which bore the calluses of war, work and hardship. Love was in the sweat on his brow, in the sacrifices made so his children could have that bike or pair of shoes. Love shined from his face on all those Christmas mornings as we opened the gifts he worked so hard to buy. It was in the family dinners around the kitchen table, even when he made us eat all our vegetables. My Dad never spoke much, he wasn't good at verbal communication, but he was always there for us. A week later his life journey was complete. My Mum, my niece Crystal and I sat at his bedside and watched him peacefully sleep away. God bestowed upon us strength, peace and comfort for the loss we have felt. God has a way of changing our perspective.

Now I not only know, but I accept my Father's love. I realized just how much I loved him. I miss his unspoken love and I miss him being part of our lives. I do not know why it took me so long to realize that love. Was it too late? No. Some people never find that love. It dies along with the person.

When God does remove that bandage, he removes the scales from our eyes. I could see my Dad through the eyes of Jesus. Love became a reality instead of a dream. Time is short and precious, but it is never too late to remove that bandage. It is never too late to allow healing to take place. I thank God for His help and the healing He does in our lives. God is a great physician. If you have a wound covered by a bandage, go to that great Physician. Allow Him to work a miracle in your life.

Praise is to God.
In memory of John Gordon Wills
October 2000

The Bandaid
CHAPTER 3

1. What does the Bible say about forgiveness? (Exodus 34:6-7, Numbers 14:18, Palms 103:1-5, Mica 7:18-20, Matthew 6:14-15, 18:35, Luke 7:49, Ephesians 4:32)

2. What happens when a deep wound is left untreated and simply covered up? (Isaiah 53:5, 1 Cor. 2:24)

3. What characteristics do you see in God; by the way He helped the writer deal with her wounded relationship?

4. Have you ever experienced the Lord removing a bandage from one of your old wounds? Discuss your experience?

5. What steps can you take to start removing the bandages from your wounds?

6. In our walk in life, we experience contrast all the time. Examples: To gain is to lose. To live is to die. Rich must become poor. Weak are made strong and the list goes on. What are some contrasts experienced in the story? Do a bible drill and see what contrasts you can find? How do they apply to your life?

For further study:

The bible has some advice, which may help you begin, the process of healing your old wounds.

Read Genesis 37- 50. Study carefully Josephs' life. Notice the different stages his life went through: Struggles, bitterness, betrayal, forgiveness and reconciliation.

A Father's Love

She sat, arms
stretched out to her Daddy
crying out for love,
with no restriction, no restraint
at all: No walls to
divide them, complete
unconditional
love she gestured:

I love you!

II

He picked her up,
hands soft and gentle.
He held her
like a delicate flower,
you are my child.

The baby
responded with smiles:

a coo, of unknown
words, but
in his heart he knew.

III

The bond of
parent and child
grew in the realm of eternity.

By her side by day,
to protect her
by night

A scary noise
interrupts her sleep

He defends her
in the darkness of the night:
Okay
Daddy's here.

IV

Years have passed by.
She said, reminiscing
with love and gratitude within
her heart,

He loved me
unconditionally
He loved me

His gentle hands, callused
from hard work:
Never did
anyone harm

All the years
he directed my path,
with great insight
and knowledge divine.

It was like
having a constant friend.
Even still

he dwells within my heart.
There he will reside
until we meet again.

4

The Wedding Day

Balancing the trivial with the tragic

The shining sun arose. Misty dew lay upon the plush green grass. Bright yellow dandelions raised their heads, as if reaching toward the light. I awoke, stretched out my arms and yawned to prepare myself for the day ahead. Today was not like any other day, for today my life would change dramatically. Today, I would be married to my gallant knight in shining armour.

The ancient custom is that the bride does not see her groom until they meet at God's altar. The men dressed, fussed and joked, as they put on their tuxedos. Meanwhile my bridesmaids and I stayed in a little cottage, which was soon to be my permanent home. Three women and no hot water, frantically we watched the old tin pot boil as the minutes seemed to turn into hours. We drew straws to see who would get the first bath. Petty things consumed us that we thought needed to be done. My maid of honour was painting her shoes with nail polish to make them match her dress. Of course we were trying to style our hair to perfection. I was beginning to wonder if we would ever be at the church on time.

Before we went to the church, all the women gathered at

my mother's house. There, we patiently endured the long process of picture taking. It was time to go to the church. Everyone dispersed like a school of minnows when you throw a pebble into the water.

Hastily they all jumped into their sparkling clean, decorated cars and went on ahead to the church. One very important element of a wedding is the bride and her bridesmaids. Somehow in the shuffle they forgot us, and the five of us were left stranded.

One friend had excellent timing. He was driving by the house in his little blue Honda Civic when he saw us looking bewildered. He stopped the car, barely spoke the words "Can I," when we all plunged into his car, like a flock of seagulls going after a piece of bread.

By the time we arrived at the church, our dresses were quite wrinkled. We pulled each other out of the matchbox he called a car. Perspiration stains nicely decorated our burgundy dresses like embroidered flowers. What do you expect in eighty five-degree heat? It was a hot record breaking May 15th, and we were late.

Music started and the church organist played a few minors, where she should have played a few sharps. The weather-beaten bridesmaids gracefully strutted up the aisle, just the way they had rehearsed. It was my turn next. I grabbed my Dad's arm, and said, "Come on Dad." It was like they glued his feet to the floor. The evidence of a slight stroke my Dad endured a few months earlier. Arm in arm, I pulled my Dad down the aisle. We missed every beat along the way. I looked up and there he stood, my husband to be. His face was glowing with deep, sincere love flaming from his eyes. He was a portrait of perfection, with a smile so full, so radiant, so, expressive. He totally enveloped me in his love. Love consumed us as we gazed into each other's eyes. The Minister's voice became like a shadow in the distance. That is because he stopped talking and it was our turn to say our vows. Here we were two young innocent people vowing our eternal love to each other in a covenant made before God.

The candles flickered with a lucid glow. We said "I do," then my friend began to sing, "We've Only Just Begun." Her voice sounded angelic. The words struck the chords of one's soul. Piano music echoed pleasantly within the church walls.

The best man fainted from the heat, just before we were to sign the legal papers. We plunked him in a chair and undid his tie to revive him, so he could be our legal witness. That formality was completed. The un-tuned organ played triumphantly loud. The Minister announced, "ladies and gentlemen, may I introduce Mr. and Mrs. Hickson."

Tears of joy flooded the church as we exited through the church doors. Moments later we stood outside the church beneath the magnificently arranged apple blossom tree, which were in full bloom. The apple blossoms matched each of the bridesmaid's beautiful bouquets of pink and burgundy flowers. They took more pictures. My face ached from smiling. It is hard to keep smiling when you are wearing four-inch heels. I must mention the tight pantyhose and more than one hundred people flashing cameras, yelling: "smile, say cheese and look this way." Five hours of smiling makes you want to scream. I just kept reminding myself, "We have Only Just Begun to Live." We survived all the pictures, the sore feet, ringing glasses and embarrassing kisses. The evening was quickly coming to a close for us. We had left to change into our going away outfits, and then returned to the wedding party to say our goodbyes. We had just returned to the party that was full swing ahead. Joyful laughter, amusing talk, energetic dancing entertained the guests. "The Gay Gordon," an old favourite dance song, was playing.

Nonchalantly, we snuck our way into the dance, hoping

no one would notice, we had returned. The song ended, creating a pause between songs. That was when my Aunt Alma and Uncle Jack greeted us back and wished us well, with a gesture of a hug and a kiss. The pause ended and "The Gay Gordon" played for the second time. We took five steps forward, two steps back, twirled, danced ahead five steps and . . . Echoing through the hall was the sound of a heavy weight hitting the floor. We turned around and there lay Uncle Jack. The music stopped, time stood still . . . the look of disbelief, shock and panic filled many faces. Uncle Jack was deathly still. Someone tried CPR. Others ran in turmoil looking for a phone to call for help. An ambulance came and took Uncle Jack away.

Many guests left, as tears filled their eyes with grief. Others stayed and partied until the early hours of the morning. Aunt Alma did not leave though she knew Uncle Jack was dead. She had witnessed death before, when her first husband died. Aunt Alma was determined to remain at our wedding to the end. She sat and listened attentively as I sang "You Light Up My Life" to my husband Don. We saw the wedding go through the formalities. Even so, Aunt Alma was touched and comforted by the song. The song "You Light Up My Life" was Aunt Alma and Uncle Jack's favourite song. It was time to leave the wedding party. The wedding, which had taken a year to prepare, was almost over. There are some things in life we cannot plan, some things we have no control over. Mixed emotions filled the air. Our life together had just begun. Uncle Jack's life came to an abrupt end. We said our good-byes. We redefined sentimentality that evening. I was hugging and kissing people I hardly knew. Then my husband and I rode off in a white Cadillac and we have been paying the bills ever since.

The Wedding Day
CHAPTER 4

1. This story brings together the comically trivial situations in life with the sadly tragic, representing one person's view of a wedding day. Reflect on a day or event in your life and combine the trivially funny with the seriously sad?

2. "We saw the wedding go through the motions." Can you relate to this line? If you have ever felt this way, explain your situation and reaction? Describe the result?

3. Often in life, we try to plan every detail. Often something happens, which is out of our control. How should we react, when this happens? Explain.

4. Read 1 Corinthian 7. Compare "The ancient custom is that, the bride does not see her groom, until they meet at God's altar." What does the apostle Paul convey about marriage?

5. Read Genesis 2:23 for more information about the first marriage, that of Adam and Eve. Genesis 24, Abraham's servant finds a wife for his son Isaac. What do these verses tell us about marriage?

In history, as early as the book of Genesis, there was an emphasis on not marrying foreigners. Discuss possible reasons or meaning?

For further study read Judges 13, 14, 15, 16, and 17.

6. What results did Samson have in his marriage to someone from a different culture and religion?

7. What happened to Samson's wife and Father?

8. What was the result for Samson when he married a Philistine woman named Delia?

5

When Time Stands Still

❧

Enduring the numbness of death

Time stands still while a clock ticks to the beat of a hypnotic song. A line of friends converse with strangers, some with giddy laughter, as they hide their pain in the numbness of reality. Others weep at the unspoken words of love, the smile left unseen, the hug of appreciation, which never happened. All this self-reproach can be put into an empty box, in the corner of one's fading memory. A little too late are the unspoken words to the one who would have appreciated them most. Now her body sleeps, lifeless and cold, an empty shell, in a shiny wooden casket. It is similar to a snake shedding its skin. The shell remains yet the soul and spirit go to some other place.

We fill the room with a garden of flowers, but the smell of death lingers with an over-powering stench of stagnating weeds. It is a three or four-day ritual which leaves people with simple yet unanswerable questions. Whys? What ifs? Questions that gets lost in a barrage of thoughts. Time seems to stand still, while we ponder over fond memories and vivid pictures of times we shared.

The memories bring a moment of refreshing laughter,

until reality comes crashing down. A cloud burst of tears swell up from the depth of emotionalism, leaving emptiness, which wrenches the very soul. Ties are broken and lives are altered. One day or one minute can change our lives forever. Some people carry the pain not just through this day, but also with them to their own death.

Blessed is the one who can take comfort in God's promises and does not have to walk through the valley of death alone, but instead, walk hand and hand with the Author of Life. The parlour may be full of people whom their own love has blinded. They mourn an empty shell, of what was once beautiful and full of vitality. Unknown to them, Jesus has delivered her soul from her foes. She has salvation, which they granted to her through Christ Jesus. By faith she walked in God's promises, living her life after the Lord.

What happens to all the others, who pour out their sentiments onto the columns of the obituary pages? Are their lives filled with empty words and grief, which are really nothing more, then an inkblot on a page of recycled newspaper? Do they reap the joy of His salvation? Do they inherit God's promised kingdom of eternal life, a heavenly place where time stands still forever? Heaven is a place where love and perfection abounds, in the presence of a great and awesome God.

I pray all would accept His Mercy, the gift of eternal life. Simplicity at its finest, the gift is Christ Jesus, a gift waiting to be unwrapped. Open it.

When Time Stands Still
CHAPTER 5

1. (Psalm 116.) The psalmist cries out to the Lord during the darkest of trials: death, troubles and sorrow. Realizing, how precious we are to God, that death cannot steel our soul for we have salvation to walk in the land of the living. God watches over us in death. What other insights do you pick up from reading this psalm?

2. What does God's Word reveal to us about what happens after death? (Romans 5:12-21)

3. The Bible tells of a man named Lazarus, who Jesus knew quite well. Lazarus was the brother of Mary and Martha. Read Luke 10:38 and John 11:1-44. Write down important points about Mary, Martha, Lazarus and Jesus?

4. When Jesus arrived back at Bethany, He responded to Mary and Martha according to their two different personalities. How did He respond to their common statement, "If you had been here, my brother would not have died?"
(John 11:21-43)

5. What can we learn about God, and about love (God's love)?

6. How does the bible explain death?
(John 11:13, 1 Corinthians 15)

7. Why believe in life after death? Can you find more facts that would support Paul's arguments, which would convince the unbeliever of this day? Read 1 Corinthians 15.

Paul encourages us to stand firm on the basics of Christianity: Christ died for our sins, he was dead and buried, rose from the dead and appeared to many people. Christ conquered death, so death becomes a beginning, not an end to all who believe in the Saviour Jesus Christ.

6

Karyn - Who Was She?

❧

There is a wonderful painting of a shepherd, reaching over a cliff, extending His arm down over jagged rocks, to a sheep below, stranded on a rock on which it had fallen. It seems that the shepherd gathers up the sheep with ease, and brings it to safety. The arm appears strong and seems to have a divine purpose in the rescue. The sky in the backdrop is a mixture of different shades of blues with the sun shining down. The painting reminds me of our dear friend Karyn. She was an artist who enjoyed portraying her relationship with her Saviour in her paintings. She often used a blend of different colours - each shade having a purpose - each stroke of her artist's brush almost a picture in itself. People would look deeply into her paintings, seeking the hidden meanings. Or maybe they just looked too deeply. Sometimes we need to look at life the way we might look at Karyn's paintings. If we look with spiritual eyes, we can see more clearly and gain more understanding. If we look with spiritual eyes we can see and understand the Artist and His masterpiece of life and death. Karyn not only looked with spiritual eyes, she painted with a spiritual heart. Karyn's paintings expressed her love and passion for Jesus. I attended Karyn's last art show. To look at her paintings and hear her explain to the audience the meaning of each painting drew me deeper into whom Karyn really was. More than anything her paintings showed me how deep her love was for the Lord. Karyn said, "My inspiration comes from the Lord." She was a visual missionary.

Her mission was to see others come into her kind of loving relationship with her Saviour, through her art.

Karyn could appreciate the finest detail of the creator - the greatest artist of all. As she walked in the outdoors or worked in her garden, she bathed in God's awesome creation. For Karyn, walking in God's creation was like breathing the very breath of God. She was an avid hiker for many years, and marked many trails with her praises to God. To her the outdoors was a place of refreshment, inspiration and solitude. It was a place where she could feel His presence in the wind or in the stillness of the summer air. She could hear His song as a natural symphony of birds and frogs, as if God was singing a love song just for her. No wonder Karyn also loved to go hiking with her friends and share God's love with them. When I think of Karyn I see every day as being a new trail for her to experience.

Karyn fell to her death while hiking one of those trails her steps had graced so often. She was taking a picture and, like the sheep in the painting, fell off a cliff to the ground. This would be the last picture she would take, remembrance of which will be forever in our hearts.

In temporal terms Karyn was a mother, wife, daughter, sister and friend. She had the gift of encouragement - she didn't strive to encourage others - she just did it as easily as painting her pictures. She was a hug and a kiss to brighten your day. The consensus at the funeral was that she had a way of making people feel special. An amazing number of people who attended her funeral told many stories of lives touched in a meaningful way. One person after another sang her praises. Obviously I was not the only one Karyn had made feel special. Most Sunday morning's Karyn greeted me with a hug and a kiss on the cheek with a sincere 'hello'. She was genuinely interested in how people were doing.

There are all too few people like Karyn, who have the gift of encouraging others and who apply that gift to all those they meet.

Church can be a busy place at times. I know that I am guilty of not always making time for others. Karyn has left me with a valuable lesson, and a challenge - the same challenge Jesus has put before each of us. It is sad that it takes something as tragic as a death to make people, like myself, take notice and want to be a better person. However, we must be careful not to allow the guilt to overtake the reality of the fact that everyone has different qualities and gifts. We should examine ourselves in the right perspective, realizing there is always room for improvement. At a family retreat a month before her death, Karyn noticed my brand new hiking boots. She showed me her worn out old boots and said she needed to get a new pair. I believe Karyn has her new set of boots now. As for me, I believe I'm just starting down some new trails of life. Karyn and I went on one little hike together, which will always remain special. My regret is that we didn't get to go on more - that I didn't get to know her to a greater extent. We must learn from our regrets - that is part of the growing process. I thank God for the times we did share.

Karyn kept a journal of prayers and thoughts for all the people that passed through her life. The day Karyn was taken away, she had finished her last page in her journal book. One blank page remained. I think our pastor said it best, "God is going to write the last page." We find it difficult to comprehend why God would take her home, when she had so many dreams she wanted to fulfill. Lives have already been changed by her life and her death. Karyn is with the Lord Jesus now, yet she lives on in many ways, through all the lives she has touched.

When I think of Karyn I am reminded of the painting of the shepherd and the sheep. I believe that the Shepherd reached down to his sheep, Karyn, and lovingly carried her into His eternal studio, where two artists will create something beautiful together. Maybe they are painting those places prepared for us - how beautiful they will be! When we join them, Karyn will be waiting with her big bright smile, shining eyes and a big, loving hug.

Karyn Percival 1950 - 2000

Who was she?
An extension of God's love.

"Those who walk uprightly enter into peace;
they find rest as they lie in death."
Isaiah 57:2

Karyn
CHAPTER 6

Karyn is a child of God, someone who loves Jesus passionately. We know that Karyn appreciated the beauty in everything God created. Let us step into praise with the psalmist and praise God for all things.

1. Read and pray Psalm 148 and ask the Holy Spirit to open the eyes of your heart to see and experience His presence and lead you into worship. Write a journal of your experience with God. Write your feelings, emotions and your prayers.

2. Praise God in Psalm 150. With Instruments, music and dancing.

3. Do a little assignment of your own by studying Psalm 145 and put your creative gifts into motion. Paint a picture or write a poem or a song, which will give praise to the Lord. May that same inspiration that touched Karyn to paint such beautiful paintings, also inspire you.

7

Awakening
Prayer of Praise

❧

Eyes wide open

Awaken one more day to the sound of singing birds, fresh air filtering through the rustic screen window. Awaken another day to God's majestic voice. Across the lake God welcomes us with open arms. The rising sun slowly peaks, stretching an endless ray across the mirror-like water. Sleepy eyes and refreshed smiles greet the day. Musical orchestrations project a peaceful song from the elements of wind, water, and trees. Clouds dance gracefully beneath the enchanting sky. My eyes behold a panoramic painting that captures the essence of creation. In awe I look, wide-eyed, amazed at the originality of God's creative masterpiece. Fragrant and sweet is the blend of trees and wild flowers. Trickling water showers down from a water fall, beckoning us. Water comes forth, splashing over the rocky terrain. The rock's face gushes with laughter, as water squeezes through the cracks and crevices. Cascading water pounds the rocks below, creating a steamy mist of authentic tranquillity.

Touched again by God's majestic hand. Soaking up His Grace poured out upon us like sweet milk and honey. Such joy and laughter echo in the distance, as our hearts sing out with love and gratitude to our great creator.

O Lord, forever lavish your spring of water upon us.
O Lord, forever cleanse us, shower us with your mist.
O Lord, forever quench the thirst within us, with the river of water leading to eternal life.

Awakening
CHAPTER 7

1. This poetic picture of words, exalts God for the beauty of His creation. Paint your own descriptive picture; about the wonderful provisions God has surrounded you.

2. The end of the poem is a prayer, for a continual spring of water poured fourth. What kind of water does scripture tell us we need? Why do we need this kind of water? (Psalm 46-4, John 4:10-15, 7:37-41, Revelation 22:1-2)

3. What does Revelation 22:1-2 say about the River of Life? Study any footnotes. What parallels can you find, about the description of the Garden of Eden, within the first three chapters of Genesis and the last two chapters of Revelation?

4. What does this chapter Awakening, say about the water of life?

The Lake Front By
The Moonlight

By the lake front,
 a beautiful vision
  of shimmering stars
   and moonlight
     disperse a vivid image,
      across the lake.
        Water ripples, rhythmically,
       as the wind whistles,
      creating music in the air.
There is a reflection
of the moon and stars,
  dancing vigorously,
    across the serene water.
      Quiet and fresh,
        the air has a fragrance,
         of nature's perfumes.
        Enveloped by peace,
       as the mind flashes pictures,
    to be stored
      in a book of memories,
        of the lake front
          under the moonlight.

His Mercy

There I sat watching out the window,
Like a blue jay going to and fro.
Silence was surrounding me.
Emptiness consumed my soul.

Lord Jesus help me.
Give me light so I can see.
Spirit guide and direct me.
Paint the path that will set me free.

Father I know I'm not perfect,
Though at times I pretend to be.
I know you're the One,
Who is brighter then the sun.
You are the key to eternity.

The Lord Jesus helped me.
He gave me light, now I can see.
His light flickers before me.
Now I have life for eternity.

Thank you Father for all your mercy.
Thank you Father for all you've done for me.
For the moon, the sun,
The stars that light the night.
Most of all the sacrifice of your Son's life.

His Mercy

1. Salvation is the deliverance from danger or evil; especially deliverance from all that separates people from God. Salvation is the key to eternity. What do these scripture references reveal? (Romans 5:6-11, 10:1-13, Acts 16:16-34).

2. Can you remember the first time you prayed to the Lord? If asked to write a song about your experience, what would you say in the song? How were you feeling at the time?

3. What was the outcome of that prayer? How has your life changed since your prayer?

4. What things in your life can you thank your Heavenly Father for giving to you?

8

When God Lights a Fire

❦

Finding refuge

The force of the wind pulled out our hair, made our eyes water and our lips flutter. We skimmed over the calm water like a bouncing pebble.

Suddenly the boat came to an abrupt stop. Billows of black smoke puffed from the engine. We were without a proper paddle and no waves to propel us. In the darkness of the night, we sat confined to the boat, feeling quite helpless.

The skipper of the boat thought he should light a flare, to signal for help. "That was a great idea," I thought. But then I noticed the Skipper fumbling around in the dark, trying to find a lighter. He then tried to read the flare directions. His hands shook nervously. Noticing the Skipper's lack of confidence, I became quite nervous too. That was when I crawled cowardly through a tiny door in front of the boat. I thought for sure I would find refuge there. Within seconds the skipper lit the flare. It shot out of his hand like a rocket, landing right back into the boat. Sparks dispersed and fire ignited the boat seat and the carpet in front of my escape hatch.

Frozen by fear, powerlessly dismayed, I stared, through the flames. Curled up like a helpless little baby, I was thinking, "this is the end of life as I know it." My pondering thought, "Will it be heaven or hell?"

Thinking that at any moment the boat would explode into many fragments, I asked God for forgiveness of my sins and asked Jesus for help. Instantaneously, a little voice inside said: "It will not be either. Take that pillow and put out the fire."

I was tired of watching the other passengers' feeble attempts to put out the fire. I leaped up from that cowering position, as if released from a deathly grip. With the tightly clutched pillow in hand I began to flail at the flame. A voice yelled, "Don't, you will spread the fire." Determination ignored the words spoken. Down came the pillow and after a couple of swipes at the fire, it dwindled its last breath. I smothered it. "Ha! Take that!" The fire was out, reduced to a smouldering puff of smoke.

The Skipper had some repairs to make to his hot speedboat. (Pun intended). There was still another flare to light. The Skipper held the flare in his blistered hand. With the flare facing the right direction, he lit the flare and up into the sky it flew. Someone standing on shore spotted the cry for help. A police boat came to our rescue within minutes. After we gave our embarrassing account of the nights events, they towed us to shore.

Reflecting back, I can see how God answered my distress-call. I can laugh about the situation in which I found myself. God has a sense of humour. He knew I needed a little fire lit, not only to accept Jesus Christ, but also to walk with Him into the waters of Baptism. I realized I needed to change many things in my life and start living a life that would bring honour and glory to my Saviour. Three months later I was baptized and my life has changed. Jesus has put my feet on a new journey through life. This journey I don't walk alone. He still calms the storms and helps me put out the fires. Perhaps God is lighting a fire in your life? The water of life (Jesus) can put out your fire. "Get up and put out that fire."

When God Lights a Fire
CHAPTER 8

1. Have you ever felt like you were riding the fast road of life, totally in control, having the time of your life, than wham, your engine is shut down? How did you respond? What is the outcome of your story? Where did you turn for help?

   Deuteronomy 33:27 "The Eternal God is your refuge, and underneath are everlasting arms."

2. In the Bible, we are directed approximately twenty-three times to a place of refuge.
   Research (Deuteronomy 33:27,
   2 Samuel 22:3, 22:31, Psalms 2:12, 9:9, 46:1,91:2)

3. In studying the previous scripture references, we learn the Lord is our refuge. He is also our strength, our rock of foundation, a shield and our fortress. Blessed are those who take refuge in God. Define the full meaning of these words?

For further study:

4. In 2 Samuel 22, David sang to the Lord the words of this song, recognizing the Lord delivered him from the hand of all his enemies, including Saul. Study the entire chapter, then write down all the verses, which come alive to you, relating to your circumstance or to the story When God lights a Fire?

Example:

2 Sam 22:1-7 David's distress call answered vs
The answered distress-call in the chapter about the fire on the boat.

9

When Hope Conquers The Elements

Finding hope through blurred vision

Once upon a time, there was a little girl named Lisa who lived in the country. Lisa had no friends or neighbours. Everyday Lisa would go outside into her big back yard. Her father was a carpenter. He built her a great big jungle gym with many swings, a teeter-totter and a couple tires. In her back yard she also had a dollhouse. They decorated it with flowered curtains, a table, chairs, sofa and a colour television. A secret door was built into the ceiling that leads to the attic. This was Lisa's secret hideout. This was a place Lisa would spend hours upon hours playing with her stuffed animals, Slinky the cat and Rusty the dog.

One day a girl named Samantha moved into an old log cabin found down the road from Lisa's big beautiful house. Samantha was a very quiet, shy girl. Her family was very poor. Samantha had no toys, no dolls and no television. Every day she would go outside into her small backyard. Samantha would talk to the flowers, trees, and the small animals. Chippy the chipmunk would eat acorns out of Samantha's hand. She would giggle happily as Chippy tickled her hand with his whiskers. She would climb the trees with an abundance of energy, always smiling.

One day Samantha was walking down a path talking to the flowers along the way. Samantha was so enveloped in her play she strayed into Lisa's backyard. Samantha looked around and noticed the beautiful dollhouse. It was like nothing she had ever seen before. The spectacular sight her eyes beheld captured her.

Curiously, she crept closer and closer to the dollhouse, until she was right at the door. Samantha spoke tenderly to the flowers on the windowsill. Her eyes glazed with excitement. Lisa was inside the dollhouse and heard the tiny little voice outside. Lisa slowly pulled back the curtain and peaked through the window with one eye. "Who is this stranger?" She wondered. Lisa watched Samantha for a little while, studying her every move. Clouds began to cover the sky and the wind began to blow with a great force. The tree branches were bending violently. Leaves were flying through the air. The swings crashed against each other. Samantha looked around and discovered she was not sure of her way back home. The wind began to frighten her. Her smile turned to a frown. She sat herself down on the step of the dollhouse. Her eyes fought back the sting of water, and then she folded her head into her hands and cried heart-wrenching tears.

Lisa heard the little girl's sobs. Her heart was filled with empathy. With blurred vision Samantha lifted her head in one final desperate hope that she might see her way home. The door behind her creaked as it opened. Samantha jumped back startled by the movement. Cautiously Samantha looked into the dollhouse through the opened door. Slowly Lisa peeked around the door! "Would you like to come in out of the storm?" Lisa asked. Samantha looked up at Lisa with a curious look, and then with an expression of sincere gratitude

Samantha said, "Yes, I would like to come in out of the storm." Inside the dollhouse Samantha ventured.

On that stormy day sunshine spread across the valley. Two strangers became best friends. Together they played every day sharing with each other blessings. They would climb the trees, and pretend to ascend the highest mountain. They would play in the dollhouse, sip pretend tea, and talk to Slinky the cat and Rusty the dog. Whatever they did together they did with love, truth, dignity and honour. The moral of the story is that the best of friendships are made with a childlike heart. Model Christ like friendship and your friendships will be an extension of His friendship to one another and to you also.

Can you relate to Samantha? Are you feeling like a lost child, like there is a storm raging around you? There is hope. Unlike fictional characters like Samantha and Lisa, you can drink from a real cup. You can ascend the highest mountain in life. Take comfort in knowing Jesus Christ is waiting to give you shelter. He is willing to bring you in from the storm. Don't be afraid to knock on the door of that little dollhouse. Inside you will find a best friend, a friend for life.

"Psalm 91 - He is my refuge and my fortress, my God, in whom I trust."

If you are someone who has struggled with lasting friendships, you might relate to my story. It has been my experience that Jesus is that best friend. Through the devastatingly painful times and rampant emotions caused by rejection and broken friendships, God has given me strength to carry on. He has always drawn me spiritually closer to Him in the process. I would like to encourage you to go forward and always put your hope in Jesus first and foremost. Allow yourself to discover God's love, compassion and forgiveness extended to you as you cope with your disappointments. Even to His death, Jesus was also rejected by His friends. In my pain I have gained empathy for the pain

Jesus also must have felt. Realizing, I have been one of those friends that has time and time again hurt Jesus, the same way that my friends have hurt me. While you may feel the same pain, you will learn God's greater love for you. It is a painful lesson, but God's perfect love will be your reward. Loyal friendships are possible. There are many examples in the Bible. That is an awesome revelation to become a reality in your personal relationship with the Lord. May God bless you with a friend like Samantha, while never forgetting that Jesus is the best friend you will ever have?

When Hope Conquers the Elements
CHAPTER 9

1. What similarities or contrasts, do you see between Lisa and Samantha?

2. What was Lisa and Samantha's reaction to the storm? What are some reactions you have had, to a stormy situation in your life?

3. How does Lisa's reaction to Samantha's crisis, parallel to some responses, Jesus gave to people in crisis? Study some biblical examples? (Luke 8:22-25, Job 38, Psalm 107:29.

4. List some of your favourite scriptures, which have brought you comfort in your trials?

5. In what ways, have you experienced God's hand or love in your life, during your personal trials? Did you experience any growth or revelation while going through problems?

6. Samantha and Lisa became best of friends. In real life, is a friendship like Lisa and Samantha's fairytale friendship, a realistic expectation? What does the Bible say about friendship or how we should treat other people? Reference (Proverbs 3:27-28; 16:28; 17:9,17; 18:24; 27:6,10; Matthew 11:19; Luke 11:8; John 15:13-14; 19:12; James 2:23; 4:4)

7. Can you find a moral to this story? What did you learn from this study?

8. For further study:

9. Study Proverbs 27:10. What parallels and contrasts can you find between the story <u>When Hope Conquers the Elements</u> and the Proverb?

There is hope

Life brings so
many questions
with the trials
of our lives.
Questions of
death, sickness
and strife.
In a world where there seems to be no answers.
There is hope. There is hope. You'll find the hope
in the Holy Bible.
For the answers
are there on
every page.
The words are
inspired by God's
own hand
Promises fulfilled
from age to age.

(Jesus brings us hope)

10

In Silence - Hope

❧

God answers a timid prayer

Sirens screamed and red lights flashed, as the ambulance pulled into the emergency parking lot at the hospital. It was an otherwise quiet Sunday afternoon near the end of summer. Summer is supposed to involve fun, swimming, barbeques and gentle breezes. Our lives were transformed that day quickly as the changing wind.

The telephone rang. It had a peculiar ring. A ring that speaks in a tone we hesitate to answer. Somehow we just know the news is not good. Perhaps it is the deafening silence that hangs on the other end, when we say "Hello!"

On the other end of the phone was my brother's voice. Dismayed, nervous, he cleared his throat before departing the news. His fifteen-year-old son was in a coma. Trying to be controlled, my brother tried to explain to me the doctor's diagnosis. Jason had a form of Bacterial Meningitis that caused three blood clots on his brain, paralysing the left side of his body. Doctors were not really sure how to treat Jason because his sicknesses were very unusual. All we really knew were that Jason was in a coma and death was knocking on his door.

A strange sense of wonder, frustration, comes over you when someone close to you is dying. All our hope, was in the hands of the doctors. That brought very little comfort, as they were grasping at straws too. Doctors gave us very little hope that Jason would even live through the night. Somehow! It humbles the proudest of people to pray. Somehow a little seed was watered; a seed that was planted years ago in a little two-room Sunday school class. After being forgotten for many years a seed of hope began to sprout - the sprout reached up into the heavenly realm. With every ounce of sincerity in our hearts we prayed. Broken tears stained our clothing. Our contrite hearts wept a prayer of tears that spoke volumes. "God, please heal Jason." It was a timid prayer yet sincere, a simple prayer yet meaningful. Was it an amazing prayer? Some would say not. However, the answer to that prayer was amazing. God revealed His power by his merciful healing hand.

Four days later our emotional roller coaster began to slow. The phone rang. It had that peculiar ring. Silence hung on the other end. The solemn tone of disbelief hung in the air like a lead balloon. "I have some bad news." Stated my mother. "Is it Jason?" I asked. "No! Jason's doing much better . . . It is your brother Larry. He died in his sleep today." The silence of that phone call of Larry's death, for months prompted many questions - questions, which in essence lead me to a personal relationship with my Lord Jesus Christ. My brother's death birthed spiritual life into me. God's ways are mysterious but always work for good.

Jason came out of the coma the same week Larry died. He had some paralysis to overcome. After three months of intensive therapy, Jason went back to school. I believe God answered our prayers and in doing so watered many dying seeds.

My brother Larry did not have anyone praying for him. He told me that week; he had a cold and couldn't seem to shake it. "It's just a cold," I thought. "Big brother will be fine." We allowed no time to pray for him, we were so worried about Jason. There was no time to prepare for Larry's death. Like many others, I believe Larry also prayed for Jason. Larry was feeling bad about Jason and I believe in my heart, Larry would have taken Jason's place if he could. Larry was one of the most sentimental men I have ever met. He had a rare compassion and love for family and friends. He was not afraid to cry. He was tall dark and handsome and one of the coolest people I've known. Larry maintained nerves of steel when He raced His speedboats. He had a rare outward confidence about himself. He would say he was #1. I think he needed to believe that outwardly because inwardly he had always struggled to express who he really was. Larry also carried a lot of pain from his past, left from the memory of the death of his first wife and then the divorce from his second wife. He had his crutch.

Sometimes people look for different ways to cope with life. For some people it may be an addiction to alcohol, drugs, or pornography. For others it could be a variety of obsessive behaviour.

Larry was my big brother and I loved him dearly. We had many talks about God. He once gave me a book to read about Jesus. One late night, just him and his sadness, Larry sat and watched 100 Huntley Street. He phoned our mother about midnight just to tell her he had been watching this tv show and that he got down on his knees and said a prayer. I do not know if Larry accepted the Lord Jesus Christ as his Saviour in that prayer? It is between him and the Lord now.

Is Jesus your Saviour? Take a moment of peaceful silence to ponder this meaningful question. If the answer is no, please take a moment to pray while you have that moment. After my brother Larry's death, I spent much time pondering many questions. Some answers were given to me when I accepted Lord Jesus as my Saviour and friend. I know someday, like Larry and like you, I will stand before God, and then I can ask God any questions I may have. God showed me the way to eternal life through my brother's death.

Whatever circumstance, struggle or persecution we may suffer, the outcome is victory, through Jesus Christ our Lord.

From Genesis, the beginning book of the bible, sin, evil and rebellion seemed to defeat humanity. The last book of the bible, Revelation shows us the long battle will end well. It reveals promises for a new creation of a perfect world without death, mourning, crying or pain. "To him who overcomes let him have an ear to what the Spirit of God has to say."

In memory of Larry Wills
September 3, 1989

In Silence - Hope
CHAPTER 10

Hope is the combination of expectation and desire, a feeling of trust. To set one's hope on something or doing something, where there may seem a glimmer of hope. Hoping against all odds, a person or things that give cause for hope.

1. What did you learn from the story In Silence - Hope?

2. The poem "There is Hope" tells us where we can find hope. Read Jeremiah 30:1-11. What word does God give Jeremiah concerning Israel and Judah, which would give them hope for the future? (Read any footnotes)

3. Read Jeremiah 30:12-24. The Lord speaks harshly, addressing the state of the people's heart, incurable wounds, injury beyond healing, no remedy for your sore, no healing etc., a very dismal picture. Verse 16 and 17 give the only hope, when God says: "But I will restore you to health and heal your wounds." Who is the enemy in your personal battle? What sins are in your life, which you need to ask God for forgiveness? What hope does God give Jacob's tent?

4. Write down your personal prayers or questions, which you may have, concerning your life circumstance. Ask God for understanding, as you read the bible to find the answers? Write down any answers, which breaths hope into your situation.

For further study:

5. Read Lamentations 3:1-33. Job, Jeremiah and Jesus suffered pain and felt God had turned His back on them. They all survived, holding onto the hope offered by God. The writer of Lamentations acknowledges the Lord's great love. He holds onto the hope offered by God. In their trials was a time to meditate and accept their grief and discover God's unfailing love. What is the best advice given to someone, who relates to the trials of the prophets of the Bible?
(Lamentations 3:22-41)

11

The Water's Edge

❧

Sitting on a rock at the water's edge of a silent bay. Peppermint greens melt with different shades of cedars and maple trees. They hung lazily over the shore's edge. Within the stillness of the calm cool water, a mirrored reflection of the landscape complemented the scenery. Minerals of white and black quarts sparkled from the rocks as the sun's lucid rays cut through the humid air. I embraced the perfection of the creator's masterpiece.

Suddenly an unusual sight gripped my eyes. I noticed a middle-aged red pine tree had been blown over by the wind. Curiosity sparked my interest, so I looked a little closer. In doing so, I noticed the broken roots that for many years had held desperately to the rocky moss surface. I wondered how this tree managed to stand upright for so long with very little soil to nourish it. Then I began to notice so many other trees bravely trying to squeeze through the cracks and crevices. Watching them reach toward the sky, I realized it is just a matter of time before they too, would get big and heavy. Eventually they would fall over to meet their death. Are we much like the trees? What do we root our stability on . . . money, business, works? If these things are our soil or foundation, will they sustain us when a heavy windstorm comes? Will we collapse in the lap of luxury?

Will we be surprised to find that our roots have been pulled out of the ground, severing the nutrients to sustain life? The richest soil I know can be found in the cornerstone. This is a rock solid surface, yes. The cornerstone of all civilization is the Lord Jesus Christ. He offers an everlasting soil, watered daily by God's word. It is a foundation that cannot be shaken, no matter how hard the winds blow. What foundation would be the best choice? The sound of sweet voices broke my deep thought. A few children came running down to the water's edge. They were full of energy and joyful laughter. I could tell it was their first time to the water's edge. They were so enthusiastic.

"Oh look at that Sammy."

"Look, look, the water is so clear."

"Wally! Look at the stones."

"Never mind that, lets go in the water."

Suddenly their enthusiasm became ambivalent as they stopped at the water's edge. Many queries entered their mind. How deep is the water? Is it cold? Are there any sharks? One by one they touched the water with their toes. One by one they jumped into the water dismissing any queries. Enthusiasm and excitement returned to their faces. Water splashed into the air dispersing droplets like a misty ocean spray.

If you feel like you are in a silent bay, remember you are not alone. Jesus calms the storms. He walked upon that silent bay often. He is the cornerstone and the Lord Jesus Christ - the Saviour. Sometimes He calls us to visit the silent bay so we will take time to listen to his voice. An old cliché, "silence speaks louder than words."

The Water's Edge
CHAPTER 11
Building a strong foundation

1. What kind of soil are your roots planted?

2. The cornerstone is the strongest point of the foundation, of which holds up, the building or structure. It is an indispensable part. How does scripture define the word cornerstone? (Job 38:6, Isaiah 28:16, Jeremiah 51:26, Zechariah 10:4, Ephesians 2:19)

3. Read through 1 Peter 2:1-12. What is the capstone? What are other names referring to Christians?

4. Whom is the living stone rejected by men? Who are the living stones today? Who is the corner stone?

5. Realizing your foundation, how are Christians to live among the pagans? (1 Corinthians 3:10-16, chapter 4)

For further study:

6. What contrast does, "The Parable of the Sower" have with the "Red Pine Tree, blown over by the wind?" (Study Mark 4:1-20, Matthew 13:1-15, 18-23; Luke 8:4-15)

7. Matthew, Mark and Luke, are three different writers but tell the same parables. Example: "Parable of the Sower," which Jesus himself told them. Write any differences in their version, of what they wrote, from hearing the parable from Jesus?

12

The Silent Bay

❧

Combating the waves with cooperation

There is a silent bay. Perhaps you have been there, to escape the hustle and bustle. It is a place I visit often. Elevated high, hidden by tall plush trees, I sat on a granite rock overlooking my silent bay. My eyes absorbed the beauty of the quiet desolate landscape. The silence hung in the air. There were no automobiles or sirens and no noise to pollute the moment. I was embodied by peace, swept up in a natural environment. Are you with me so far?

The sound of trickling water began to beckon to me. I turned my attention to see what was breaking the silence. Drips of water droplets delicately fell into the silent bay as a little red canoe paddled with the wind. Gracefully it was paddled with two synchronized strokes. The canoe glided across the water toward me. I thought how expertise the two canoeists looked because their strokes complemented each other.

Moments later the canoe turned around to venture back across the blue water to their original destination. This time the canoe was fighting against the waves and the changing wind. The canoeist's paddles plunged desperately hard into the water trying to keep the canoe on course. The harder they tried the more they lost control of where the canoe was going. Within minutes the canoeists found themselves being pushed by the waves of the water toward the rocky shore. The canoe began to rock stubbornly. Tiredness and fear fed their tension. I could hear them yelling at each other while paddling aimlessly.

In their desperate struggle they seemed to forget how to work together. They were fighting against each other more than they were combating the waves and wind. Then they did something that surprised me. You see! I was expecting them to capsize at any moment. Instead they stopped paddling, collected their composure and began paddling the canoe with synchronized strokes. Determination and cooperation helped them pick up a crosswind. The canoe moved forward cutting the waves like a blade. Conquering the wind, they reached the distant shore within minutes.

Life can be somewhat like a canoe ride down a silent bay. Sometimes we want to just paddle the side of the canoe that we feel most comfortable with. If we come up against a strong wind, we may be forced to paddle on the other side of the canoe for a while. It may be a struggle and suffering we may have to endure. With a little reconditioning the end result will be positive. You will be made stronger in your weakness. Roman 5:3-5

"Not only so, but we also rejoice in our sufferings, because we know that suffering produces perseverance; perseverance, character; and character, hope. And hope does not disappoint us, because God has poured out his love into our hearts by the Holy Spirit, whom He has given us." We must remember God is the real navigator of our canoe or lifeboat. If we don't paddle the same way God paddles, our lives can seem out of control or lacking direction. That is okay if you want to spend your life riding the rapids at Niagara Falls.

From a positive perspective, how does this sound? Flowing down a calm stream synchronously. Does it sound rather pleasant? Try consideration, cooperation and diligent work. Find the same focus and strategy as the navigator. It works even better when both canoeists adopt His strategy. This will get you to the nicest destination in life. With God as your navigator you will want to visit your silent bay quite often, I do.

The Silent Bay
CHAPTER 12

1. Write a descriptive paragraph about your personal "silent bay."

2. What does the Bible tell us about working together? (1Corinthians 12:12, Ps 133, John 17:23,Romans 15:5, Eph 4:2-3, 4:11-13, Col 3:14)

3. What insight can we gain from the story "The Silent Bay?"

4. Who is the navigator of your lifeboat or little red canoe? List some experiences, where you had to rely on the navigator (God)?

5. List your strengths and weaknesses. Think of ways to strengthen your weakness?

For further study: Nehemiah chapters 1-3

6. What steps did Nehemiah take to begin the process of rebuilding the wall of Jerusalem?

7. (Chapter 2:11-20) Who worked together with Nehemiah? What opposition did Nehemiah encounter?

8. In Nehemiah chapter three, notice, how many people were involved in working together under the direction of Nehemiah? Who was the main navigator?

9. (Chapter 3) Shows more opposition to rebuilding the wall. What did they endure? What were Nehemiah and the Israelites response to the opposition? (Nehemiah 4:6-9; 13:15,16)

   Read the rest of Nehemiah; find the result of working together in cooperation with others and with God.

A Reflection of His Love

I Praise You Lord
My trust is in you alone Lord.
You direct my path.
You make complete my soul.

With you Lord, I am forever free.
Your Love sustains me.
Continuously mending my broken heart.
Moulding me, conforming me to Your Perfect Image.

Day to day, You fill my cup with Love, and Hope.
Your gracious love and healing touch soothes my soul.
Like broken pottery restored by a potter's hand,
You restore me. I Praise You Lord

May the mountains, You have helped me climb,
return to You the pleasant fragrance of Your perfume.
Blend it with the flowers of my love,
so we can be one in Spirit eternally.

Like flowing streams,
which trickle through thick forest glades
eroding through rugged mountains,
You direct my crooked paths, always bringing me back to You.

Your tender mercies flow upon me like a cascade.
Washing me again and again.
Though 2000 years ago, Your blood was shed for me,
Your blood still flows from that cross today.

Still cleansing me.
Forever lifting my feet upon a solid rock
Reminding me of the Great Sacrificial Love,
You have always shown me.

No other Love can compare to Your Perfect Love.
Thank - You Jesus.

13

Be Still

༭

Getting to know God

Psalm 46:10 "Be still, and know that I am God"

At least three times in the Bible, God tells us to be still. He even said to the waves, *"Quiet! Be still!"* I'm a true believer that anything God says is for our own good. In this fast moving lifestyle we live in today, to be still may be easier said than done. You may ask, why does God want us to be still? What should we do when we are to be still? It has been my experience that while being still or quiet, everything around us becomes magnified. I sat on my comfortable couch one day and closed my eyes. I was amazed at the different noises I heard which I normally take for granted: Noises that get lost in my busy schedule. It made sense to me that occasionally being still was a good thing. Incorporating quiet time into my busy schedule became a priority. The more I practised quiet time the more I experienced, a better prayer time, and a deeper level of worship. I began to experience more intimate time with God. I found I was hearing God's voice with much more clarity than ever before. Being still before the Lord will enhance your relationship with Him. It is much better when we decide to be still before the Lord, rather than being brought to humbled obedience.

Sometimes we get so busy with our daily schedules. We forget our great Lord. This may be a surprise, but God also wants to be loved and appreciated. Like so many others, He is often left out of our busy lives. God above anyone else deserves recognition. Be still and know that He is God.

Be Still

CHAPTER 13

Read Nehemiah 9

1. (Nehemiah 9:5-26) We see Nehemiah's example of coming before God in prayer. Describe the way the Israelites prayed?

2. What are some things in your life, you can praise God for?

3. (Nehemiah 9:26-36) What disobedient and rebellious things did the Israelites do against God? What pattern do you notice in the Israelites behaviour?

4. What pattern do we see in God's reaction to the Israelites?

5. In what ways have you left God out of your life? Apply what you have studied about the Israelites, to your personal relationship with God. Fit God into your schedule by: prayer, meditation, study and listening for God's instruction?

6. Read the following scripture references used for the word still. (Joshua 10:13, Psalm 37:7, 46:10, 89:9, Zechariah 2:13, Mark 4:39) Write down your response to each?

14

Dangling by a Thread

❧

The thread of life

Sometimes life seems to stand still, usually in a tragic circumstance like death, illness or loneliness. During times like these worldly treasures seem to overflow the chest - times when we cannot cope with normal daily functions. Picking up a dishcloth to wash last night's dishes takes more energy then aerobics. Routine chores become impossible to achieve, especially when we feel like the dishrag. Sweeping the floor is mundane and we would rather bench press 350 pounds of iron. We struggle through these days, clinging to a thread of sanity. What is the thread made of which you dangle from? Is it a thread of silk? That is okay if you own a silkworm farm. Perhaps your dangling thread is made of cotton? Cotton is not very efficient unless you have a good astringent. Is your thread is made of wool? Baaaaaad idea. Face it. All these fabrics wear out over time sending us down the drain with the dirty dishwater. Best choice is the thread of life held together by God's word (truth) and promises. This is a thread with everlasting life. (The Saviour Lord Jesus Christ). When you get days when you feel you cannot manage, the Lord can be your source of strength and encouragement. He will be your living hope in times of trouble.

"May our Lord Jesus Christ himself and God our Father, who loved us and by His grace gave us eternal encouragement and good hope, encourage your hearts and strengthen you in every good deed and word." 2 Thessalonians 2:16,17

Dangling by a Thread
CHAPTER 14

1. Do your troubles come more from your circumstances or from your own temporal weakness? What kind of help do you need from God? Ask Him in a prayer.

2. (Read Jeremiah 29:11-14). What hope and encouragement can you find in these promises God made to you?

3. (Study John 4:19-26; 7:13-19; 8:31-38; 14:5-14). What does Jesus say about truth, in these scripture references?

4. Knowing the truth, how can the thread of your life be strengthened, especially on the days you struggle?

For further study:

5. (Read 2 Timothy 2:8-26; 2 John; 3 John). What are the key points about truth?

15

My Loyal Pup
❦

"A friend loves at all times" **Proverbs** 17:17

Do you have a best friend? I believe it is human nature to desire to have a best friend or be a best friend. I was driving to church one day when something caught my eye. There was one of those church signs you read as you drive by. It often seems that the saying on the sign tugs at your heartstrings, speaking a word of truth or encouragement. It conveys a message needed which speaks exactly to the circumstance in your life at that time. This sign spoke to me as I read, "Dog is man's best friend. You can ignore your dog, yell at your dog, and treat your dog badly. Even so, your dog is the only friend who will forgive and forget, and still come running up to greet you with its tail wagging and greet you with a kiss. Your dog is genuinely excited to see you." That sign had a meaningful message for me. It made me analyze my human friendships. It also made me take a closer look at the friendship I shared with Rusty my dog.

Rusty was an original. For many years I often wondered why God would bring such a dog into my life. Surely, this dog tested my sanity. Many times he pushed me beyond self-control, into anger, making me fly off the handle. What saved Rusty's life from my wrath? It was surely God's grace and His wisdom, to have instilled such a beauty in the appearance of Rusty. Rusty was a White Shepherd with a cross of Golden Lab. His ears and his tail were always pointing heavenward. One look from those brown puppy dog eyes often repressed my anger. Rusty was always quick with a repentant bow and a sniff of his tail.

He always knew when he did wrong, but it never seemed to cure his desire for mischief. He was just always so full of energy.

Rusty was the king of skunk finding. If a skunk came on our property he quickly went to the skunk boutique and got a sample of skunk de toilet. He would be in the Guinness book of records having been sprayed eleven times over the ten years of his life. Rusty shredded three down comforters from the clothes' line, two new swimming pool covers, three bicycle seats, three pairs of shoes, and created a mind field of holes in our back yard. One hole was so big you could have driven a Volkswagen around inside of it. I think of how he would always let me know by his hysteria when a storm was coming. He wouldn't wait for me to let him in the house. No, he would jump right through the screen door. Many times it brought me to prayers of repentance for my anger, frustration and brief moments of murderous thoughts. Often I contemplated getting some kind of deliverance for my dog and then for myself.

Over the years, some of the horrific and funny stories of things Rusty did often made for some humorous conversation. But now, I feel such sadness, and a void as I see his ghost everywhere. I'd love to see a shredded comforter of down feathers flow from one end of my back yard to the neighbors, just to have Rusty here again. He was a good watchdog always letting us know when someone came in our driveway. I miss that.

For ten years he was my shadow, while the children were

at school. So many things remind me of him, things I took for granted each day. He would always walk to the clothesline with me. By my side he would stay, as he helped me water my flowers each day. I miss his happy face and wagging tail. Rusty would always come to greet me when I came home. I miss seeing his face at my sliding door. I miss him sitting under my swing as I sit and have my coffee in the morning sun.

I miss watching him run around the pool and jump up to catch bees and flies. We called Rusty the great white hunter. I can't believe how attached I had become to this dog, who tested my limits, but who always showed me his best friend qualities. He was my loyal pup, my best friend. His time drew near. Life was snatched from this beautiful creature within a blink of an eye. Struck down in an instant. His heart stopped while he made one last jump. Without warning or sign, time stood still. My husband Don and I watched Rusty fall to the ground and drift off into an everlasting sleep. Some say dogs don't go to heaven. There is nothing in scripture, which would suggest that animals have a spirit. As I helplessly watched Rusty die, I could almost sense that there was a soul that seemed to leave his body. The life and light that were in his eyes faded out, as he whimpered his last breath.

This dog had an amazing character and was very smart. Rusty had a spontaneous instinct and a loyal nature. Could it be possible that some bible scholars may be wrong in their interpretation? Just maybe when I get to heaven Rusty will greet me with his wagging tail and those ears pointing straight up. I'd love to see Rusty again with that smile he always wore on his face. We can always hope. I've never had such a loyal friend. I miss his friendship.

Every now and then I still hear a faint bark outside of my door. I find a bone he buried in my garden. The chipmunks, rabbits, skunks and raccoons often walk on my deck and drop in for some food. They too are faithful in their visits, though they are not always welcomed. I think they miss Rusty too and that game of "catch me if you can" they would play.

At times I think about getting another dog. But I'm not ready yet. I guess I still feel loyal to Rusty. I've come to think that even our pets are unique; in the same way people are unique. There is no other dog just like Rusty. I can get another dog, maybe I will someday. I'll never find another Rusty. I loved my loyal pup. I still do.

In memory of my dog, Rusty Hickson
July 11, 2003

My Loyal Pup
CHAPTER 15

1. What can we learn from our pets, which might make us better friends?

2. Share or write a story explaining how one of your pets or even the pet of someone else, did something unusual or heroic which made a difference in someone's life?

3. Can you find scripture references about pets or their eternal destiny? (Proverbs 26:11, Ecclesiastes 9:4, 2 Peter 2:22, Mt 7:6, 15:26-27)

4. Job 12:7-13. What does Job say about learning from animals?

5. What is the definition of loyal?

6. Read 1 Chronicles 29:14-21. What does this scripture say about loyalty and integrity?

16

Exploring God's Great Glory

❧

Thinking eternal

To explore God's great glory is to sift through oceans of sand beaches. A handful of sand slowly escapes through the cracks between our fingers. Witnessing some of His magnificence with our limited vision while we are yet to understand God's full plan. Yet God's infinite glory surrounds us as He shares with us his love. Giving and giving, but God Himself also wants the set time to arrive, when His perfect love will be manifest through Him to us, then through us to Him. Ultimately, we will be equally yoked with God, as He moulds us into his perfect image. All that is good, true, honourable and righteous. All that is God's love. Giving back to God in the fullness He gives to us. This is an unbreakable yoke of oneness in all aspects of life. His ultimate plan from before creation is to unveil His masterpiece in His perfect time.

The full embodiment of His glory will no longer be limited to human understanding. They will declare it in fullness, the glory of God in Heaven and on Earth.

His hands will unleash our hearts and minds, with freedom to give willingly back to God our creator the glory and love He deserves.

Rapture

A forest of splendour
hems me in.
I am not dismayed.

Precepts of my mind expand
caught in a snapshot
of colourful photographs

Civilization beckons me from a distance
faint sounds of traffic
I am not dismayed.

Blue sky comes and goes,
dispersing clouds divide
forever changing

The breeze tickles my face
beauty captures my spirit
I am not dismayed.

Water ripples elegantly across the pond
fire flies dip their wings
then play a symphony

The essence of time seems insignificant
Solitude, nature and life exist.
I am not dismayed.

An abundance of awesomeness,
I want to stay
To embrace peacefulness

In the refreshing wonder of the outdoors
I am mysteriously taken away
I am not dismayed.

17

The Girl in the Mirror

❦

"The Lord does not look at the things man looks at.
Man looks at the outward appearance,
but the LORD looks at the heart."
1 Samuel 16:7

She stood in front of the mirror, with a disappointed gander, a snarl even, at the imperfection of the young woman looking back. Whatever face she made at the woman behind the glass, the young woman made right back. There was something strange about the person looking back. She seemed a carbon copy yet opposite in a backward sort of way. It made her crazy to ponder the image any longer. It was too much of a reality, of the way life felt to her most of the time. Was she on the outside looking in or was she on the inside looking out? Both made her feel different from anyone else, like a prisoner in herself. I know of this young woman. When she was seven years old, she was invited to a friend's birthday party. Her mother made her put on a very frilly dress. She looked adorable, but she did not feel adorable. She felt very uncomfortable. The dress just didn't fit her personality. She would have rather worn her blue jeans and T-shirt. I'll give her the name Ripley. She reminds me of rippling waves on a fresh water lake, a ripple on a pond of calmness that goes on and on. Ripley is the name I give her now, for she has not always been a glistening ripple. At times in her life she has been a raging torrent of capsizing waves. There is a God who sees all things and has begun to tame the stormy waters of Ripley's life.

Ripley's Peril

The world is a cube of intertwined life
A lonesome journey
hidden meaning
Forever searching.
Busy people running here and there
Seeking a purpose
unknown motives
Forever searching
Some are trapped, isolated, in prison
Soul from Spirit
Dying self
Forever praying
This world is a Gethsemane of choices
A disappointing gander
His will
Forever striving
An unseen ruler, this God of the Universe
A trustworthy word
The truth
Forever faithful.
The silent scream, only He can hear.
A silent repose
Invisible love
Forever seeking
A world of hope
to complete His plan
A divine appointment
Thy purpose
Forever wisdom

Much like Ripley, people are made to feel they must be something they are not. God made each person different. Everyone has different fingerprints, different voices. Twins can look the same, but they are very different from each other, with different likes and dislikes. Every human being is uniquely and wonderfully made by God.

I'll continue my story about Ripley. She went to the party. She got as far as the doorstep. Inside, she heard the laughter of her friends. She knocked so quietly that no one heard her feeble little knock at the door. "Why didn't she knock louder?" You ask. Ripley didn't want her friends to see her in that pretty dress, no matter how pretty people thought she looked wearing that dress. "How could I have any fun wearing a dress?" She thought after all. Besides, Ripley was too shy and too scared to enter, with all the kids at the party. She was also late. She certainly did not want to be the focal point. Saddened, she went back home and missed out on the party. "That is absolutely crazy," one might think. Do you wonder whatever happened to that little girl?

Ripley grew into a young woman. All her fears and insecurities she had on that door step grew with her. One day Ripley met a friend, she had always hoped to find. Ripley had all this love inside her that she needed to pour out to someone, who would receive her love and then love her in return. Simply, Ripley had a need to feel loved. The problem was that the person willing to give her love, was a woman. It was not wrong for Ripley and her friend to love each other. Biblically, it is clear that we are to love one another. The passion and love they had for each other became sin when they shared their love sexually. A moral line was crossed; an invisible line, which seems to be attached to some hearts. Though it felt so right for Ripley to love someone and be loved, deep down she knew the method was so wrong. Her flesh or sinful nature would say yes, but her conscience said no.

Again that little girl felt she had to put on the little frilly dress - a dress she hated to wear. This little girl in a woman's body had to make a choice. Would she put on that little yellow dress? Or would she wear the blue jeans she loved so much? The flesh, devil and sin were master over her life. She struggled between right and wrong. She decided to put on the little yellow dress.

Years later Ripley asked Jesus to be her Saviour, friend and the God in her life. Jesus is the only one who can truly love Ripley, more than anybody could love her and meet her every need. When Jesus became her Saviour, the Holy Spirit entered Ripley's life. She continually tried to give her old nature - old self over to the control of the Holy Spirit. That was when the battle between good and evil really began. The war inside her raged like a tossing sea.

She was made to feel even more different from anyone else. No one could really understand her, though many tried. People would come into her life claiming they understood. They would befriend her for a short time, then realize they were wrong. Understanding Ripley was too draining. So, they would run the other way and slowly fade from her life. This rejection from her closest friends would repeatedly escalate her belief that she was truly different. Ripley was determined not to harden her heart. She would continue to hope for pure love, friendship and acceptance from others.

Ripley desperately needed Jesus to be the Captain of her ship. Victory would come as their ship set sail through many storms. Again-and-again, Ripley was washed by the waves. One battleship after another would come to hinder any progress, of her reaching her destination. As Ripley's ship rested, the enemy would make sneak attacks shooting underwater torpedoes. One day while the enemy attacked the bow of the ship. Ripley yelled to the Captain, much like the disciples yelled for Jesus to help them in their storm. The Captain yelled back instructions.

He said, " Ripley, you are at the wheel. I have taught you many times what you must do to fight the battle." Now you must follow my teachings.

By this time, the yellow dress was very torn from the years of battle. Frustrated and angry from her plight, she shot consecutively at the enemy ship. She let off every bit of ammunition she had at the enemy. Then she proceeded to release her frustration to the Captain in less than a respectful manner. Within minutes the sea became a blanket of calm silence as the enemy withdrew out of sight.

Her ship sat in the middle of a vast ocean of clear water and blue sky. As Ripley sat in the silence, she realized that even the Captain spoke not a word. "What did I just do?" She pondered. Fear began to brace her mind. (Did the enemy really withdraw?) She looked into the mirror on the masthead and saw the ugly reflection of herself. Ripley hated the face that was staring back. It was disfigured from the battle. She ran to her cabin and cried and travailed until her stomach ached with pain. Oh Captain, now what do I do? She lay on her bed, weary and tired as if a spell of sleepiness covered her like a blanket. Then a voice said to her, "go cut your hair." Ripley believed her hair was her glory, her femininity. It had taken so long to grow. Her hair was the only thing about herself she could accept. She stood in front of the mirror with scissors in hand and heard the voice say, "Cut it." She put the scissors up to her hair as her stomach churned. "I can't," she thought. Down went the scissors. "Cut it!" Ripley pulled her hair back, then again lifted the scissors to cut. "I can't," she thought. It took so long to grow. "Cut it." Her stomach rose up within her with a nervous apprehension. "Cut it." The scissors cut through her curly brown locks like the cutting of a paper doll. One lock after another fell to the ground until it was all gone. She stood in front of the mirror with her boyish look. She felt like she conquered yet another enemy. Perhaps it was the enemy of self? Ripley sat in thought and this is what she felt:

`Tis but the hour of my destined fate.
Casteth out before Him want or need.
Await His tender rebuff.
To know His love, His grace, His mercy.
The dawning day from sunrise to sunset.
I search for one thread of faith,
to which my weary head may rest.
O Awaken my Spirit from this dungeon of despair.
Set forth my soul in thy love and peace.
To exist to the one who shall care.
The unwise fool of pity, that is what I am.
A fool to rise, a fool to sit.
A fool to wait all day long.
A fool to breathe, or guess or question.
Thou hast made this fool I am.
Thou can transform and make me wise.
Strip from this mortal being the foolish skin,
which suffocates this bleeding flesh.
Thou art divine in power and mercy.
In a blink of an eye, a thought,
Thy Breath of life may be released.
Refresh this tainted soul.
Sprinkle thy healing mist upon this heart that lie so bare.
You see all things like a million walls with eyes.
Life's ocean is endless like eternity.
Senseless are all pondering thoughts,
like waves upon an ocean.
They stir the sand along the beaches of a mind.
Who can fathom it?
Thou sayest "BE STILL."
Thou knowest my coming and my going.
Thou knowest all things upon a troubled shore.
For thou hast made the shore and all who build upon it.

No wonder thou sayest,
Who can fathom the wisdom of God?
The wisdom of men is but foolishness.
One must trust in thy Eternal Promise.
Cast off all self.
Thou can give strength, courage and peace divine.
Grant that I may understand thy wisdom.

For days to follow, the ship stood still. The Captain remained silent. Ripley felt physically sick, as if the ship were still in a horrendous storm, yet the water was calm. Deep inside herself again she felt she had committed a terrible wrongdoing. Ripley prayed. "Captain, please forgive me for what I've done." The Captain then reassured Ripley that He would not let the ship go down, for He was still on board. He told her, "It was not wrong that you used all the ammunition supplied." But Ripley had saddened Him because of the way she misused the ammunition, when she attacked the enemy ship. Her mistake allowed the enemy to come aboard her ship and counterattack. "Just as you were told when you were a child that you couldn't have fun wearing that yellow dress, the enemy came into your cabin and told you to cut your hair. As you can see, I am still on your ship because I love you and I will not leave you. However, you must live with what you have done and come to accept yourself the way I accept you." For many days to follow, Ripley wanted desperately to wear a new frilly dress. She realized she no longer liked her boyish look with the blue jeans, T-shirt and short hair. The little yellow dress didn't make her feel right either. She began to realize that it is the outward appearance that people really look at, not what the person looks like on the inside. That bothered her very much, because if she didn't like her outward appearance, how could anyone else?

The Captain taught her a valuable lesson through cutting

her hair. He said to Ripley, "I do not see you the way people see you. I see your heart. You need to look beyond the exterior and to the inner place. That is where all the true beauty is hidden. Your security cannot come from others; they will disappoint you over time. Security comes from the Lord. When you can realize the inner beauty and goodness in yourself, then others will see it too. They will no longer look at the outer shell either.

They will recognize the real person and will love and accept you the way I have fashioned you. This acceptance will destroy the inner sin that once became an outward action of false acceptance, false love for another and from another. Your hair will grow, just as your inner beauty grows, through you then to the outer extremities of a world with limited vision."

Whether Ripley was dressed in blue jeans and a T-shirt with a short hair cut, or wearing a frilly dress, she set sail again. They are still fighting the battles together. The Captain has brought Ripley, some friendly shipmates. They are sailing the seas of life together. The Captain is navigating their ship through the ocean waves, washing Ripley again and again, until she is polished like a fine stone. Someday Ripley will become a beautiful jewel to make a rippling difference to all those who feel different.

Two Ships

Two ships sailed two distant shores,
Through the roughest of waves,
they battled the sea wars.
Days where the ravaging winds took their toll.
The dry calmness of a vast empty ocean.
A mystery to scroll.
Though withered and worn over time,
The ships remained strong
each other to find.
Waves upon waves seemed an endless feat.
Someday, somewhere, destiny,
the two ships would meet.
On a shore of the most beautiful garden of land,
the two ships ran aground,
on the whitest of sea-sand.
Their supplies were quite low from the journey thus far.
But together combined
they could travel some more.
So it was, together they would sail.
Not a journey, an adventure
they could not fail.
God was the wind behind their sails.
He is the gentle breeze,
or the gust or gale.
God is the refreshing rain
to quench the thirsty,
to heal the pain.
So peacefully sail to life's end.
At every end there is a beginning.
Two ships, two friends.

The Girl in the Mirror
CHAPTER 17

Let us find out what God says in the Bible about homosexuality. Read Leviticus 20:13. "If a man lies with a man as one lies with a woman, both of them have done what is detestable. They must be put to death; their blood will be on their own heads."

1. What does the Bible say was the penalty for such a sin?

2. Read the following scriptures and for each write down the main message God is trying to teach us? (Genesis 19:1-29, Judges 19)

   Genesis 19:1-29 reveals homosexuality was one of the major evils rampant among the inhabitants of the cities of Sodom and Gomorrah. God's judgement was fulfilled in the destruction of the cities. (Judges 19) the act of homosexual men produced a backlash of rape and murder of a concubine.

3. Write the key points from the above verses:

4. Romans 1:18-32 What is the penalty to those who continue to do these things and approve of those who practice them? (1 Corinthians 6:9-11)

5. What is the punishment for the unrighteous vs. help for the righteous? (2 Peter 2:6-10)

6. (Jude 7) "an example of the punishment of the eternal fire." Thank God that we live under an era of grace or we would have seen a judgement of this magnitude for our lives. Does this mean that because we live under grace, God ignores this type of behaviour?

   Romans 6:1 - "What shall we say, then? Shall we go on sinning so that grace may increase? By no means!"

   Romans 6:23 - "For the wages of sin is death, but the gift of God is eternal life in Christ Jesus our Lord."

We understand God's judgement against our sins. We need to also understand how much God truly loves us. John 3:16 - "For God so loved the world that he gave his one and only Son, that whoever believes in him shall not perish but have eternal life."

18

Deliverance
Allegory

❦

Victory over darkness

In the darkness of a mean dark world.
Evil dwells and uses mockery.
To confuse a snow white dove sitting on her perch.
The dove now has her wings and is learning how to fly.

Minute by minute as each day goes by,
Evil plans an attack to make the dove fall,
Into a crevice in the earth below.
The brightness of the dove hurts the devil's eye.

Minute by minute as each day goes by,
He plucks a feather from the dove,
To take away the brightness and dull her Love.

Minute by minute as each day goes by,
The frail little dove sits half bare.
No longer can she fly.
It seems Evil has won.
Out of the brightness of the Son,
Comes along Friendly White Dove,
To help her friend fly and replenish the Love.

Minute by minute as each day goes by,
One Little White Dove is soaring high
with Friendly White Dove by her side.
They swoop with the wind, up and down, as they glide.
The love and trust grows.
With such joy and excitement they fly to and fro.

The Son warms their wings.
Their feathers shine with His brightness,
as His praises they do sing.
Laughter fills the Heavens, as they bring the Harvest in.

Minute by minute as each day goes by,
Evil plans another attack to make the doves fall,
To destroy the work and confuse them all.

Minute by minute as each day goes by,
A cloud of evil fills the sky.
The doves get separated in the darkness of the cloud.
One Little White Dove cries out loud.
Minute by minute as each day goes by,
One Little White Dove waits alone.
Calling, calling, calling . . .
No longer can she fly.
Seems Evil has won.
Through a crack in the cloud,
Did appear a tiny ray of light from the Son.

Minute by minute as each day goes by.
One Little White Dove sits.
Waiting, waiting, waiting . . .
For Friendly White Dove.
To come back and soar high together again,
to heights above.

Minute by minute as each day goes by,
One Little White Dove waits, wondering,
what went wrong? Why?

Beneath the brightness of the Son.
One Little White Dove flies alone,
Doing her best to bring the harvest home.
Minute by minute as each day goes by,
The Son evaporates the cloud in the sky.
At last! One Little White Dove can see
Friendly White Dove from afar.
One Little White Dove is eager to forget
the loneliness and pain.

The joy and excitement bubbles up again..
One Little White Dove calls to Friendly White Dove.
Over here, over here, over here . . .
It seems Friendly White Dove cannot see her,
but also has a deaf ear.

Minute by minute as each day goes by,
One Little White Dove goes to Friendly White Dove.
One Little White Dove pours out her heart
with longed excitement.
Friendly White Dove has been wounded.
She is trapped by a wall of cement.

Minute by minute as each day goes by.
One Little White Dove flies high.
She sends forth a call, to Friendly White Dove,
who is working diligently behind the cement wall.
Has Friendly White Dove forgotten times shared?
This makes One Little White Dove sad and scared.
One Little White Dove hopes and prays to the Son.
That He would melt away, what Evil had done.

Minute by minute as each day goes by.
Again! One little White Dove reaches out to
Friendly White Dove to replenish the love.
In hope that once again, they could fly side by side.
Swooping with the wind, as they glide.
But One Little White Dove can't set
Friendly White Dove free.
Friendly White Dove must do it herself,
but the cement wall she does not see.

Minute by minute as each day goes by,
One Little White Dove longs for Friendly White Dove
to fly with her again, side by side.
One Little White Dove soars high
through the mountains, with the Son as her guide.
Gliding, gliding, gliding . . .
With the gentle breeze and the light
of the Son motivating her on.

Minute by minute as each day goes by
One Little White Dove flies through the morning mist.
No longer does fear and sadness subsist.
Through the mountains, danger she does conquer.
The Son shines so brightly upon her.
Minute by minute as each day goes by.
Evil did not give up the attack.
While One Little White Dove was on a mission;
a baby to save.
Evil hurled a rockslide to trap her in a cave.
The mountains did tremble.
Oh! How the earth shook.
So hard in fact, it made Friendly White Dove look.

Minute by minute as each day goes by.
The cement wall begins to crumble,
right before her eyes.
Free at last. Friendly White Dove soars high.
Noticing smoke coming from the mountainside.
Friendly White Dove flies down to see.
When she arrives,
She finds One Little White Dove in great need.
Amongst the rubble,
One Little White Dove lays lifeless,
still, battered and torn.
Ten feet away sits a lost Little One, just born.

It seems Evil has won.
Out of the brightness of the Son,
Shines a ray of light on Little One.
Down swoops Friendly White Dove.
To take care of Little One and replenish the Love.
Minute by minute as each day goes by.
Friendly White Dove is soaring high.
Little One by her side.
They swoop with the wind up and down, as they glide.

One Little White Dove's job is now done.
She has gone home to be with the Son,
Where the eternal river of life ever flows.
No more Evil. No more foes.
The sky is peaceful and serene.
A rainbow of Love goes from stream to stream.
Joy and laughter echoes in the heavens once again.
Fly! Fly! Fly with the wind my Friend.

The End

Deliverance
CHAPTER 18

1. Find the dictionary's definition for the following words: darkness, light, devil, evil, crevice?

2. The bible is full of symbolism. Find symbolism for the following words:

   darkness........John 12:35, Genesis 1: 2-4
   light...............Romans 2:19; John 1:1-16
   devil..............Revelation 12:7-12
   dove..............Gen 8:8; Matthew 3:16; 10:16
   evil................Matthew 6:13; John 17:15; Romans 12:21
                       Ephesians 5:16
   son.................Matthew 14:22-36

3. How does evil use mockery and confusion, in the allegory and in our lives? What did evil successfully accomplish? How did good prevail? Whose praises are the doves singing?

4. Why doesn't Friendly White Dove see the wall that separates her from Little White Dove?

5. Evil never seems to give up trying to destroy the doves. Just when it seems evil has won, who intervenes to help the doves? How? Why?

6. How can we combat evil in our lives? Read the entire book of Ephesians?

7. What role does Jesus have in the battle and what part do we have in the battle?

8. Who has the final victory?

9. Sometimes it seems like it takes a trembling mountain to knock down the walls of bondage, but it really takes prayer. In the allegory, Little White Dove goes home to be with Jesus. Like Friendly White Dove, we may be left to finish the mission God has begun in our lives. What is God's call on your life? Is there any lost Little Ones, who need a Friendly White Dove, like you?

19

The Lonely Ride
on the Bus

❧

You do not have to ride the bus alone

How much love will you accept? Is there a limit to love? We realize God's love for us is limitless. Daily God extends His love and grace to us. Some people gladly receive His love and then share the gift of love with others. Some take His love and run on their merry way. Others just will not accept God's gift of love at all. They reject His love because of a wall of bitterness, anger, or fear etc. Whatever the walls consist of, they can be taken down. Walls block the open walkways preventing freedom and cause unnecessary repercussions such as: love prevention and regression. These roadblocks hold back progress in human relationships because they are cloaked by denial. If one were to realize the decay in their lives eating away at any good structure, they could prayerfully knock down the wall. In any equation to solve a problem, one must first admit there is a problem. Is there a price to pay for love? Your answer may depend on how many walls are left standing around you. The highest price ever paid was by God Himself. His perfect love for a decaying people, money cannot buy.

The crucifixion death paid the price in full, by Jesus suffering on the cross. To relate to the completeness of such a love, you may have to imagine yourself allowing the one person you love most in your life to endure a suffering death. A loved one's life to save a group of strangers lives. Meanwhile, you hold the power to intervene anytime. Can we even begin to fathom such a dying love for another? God paid the price with His perfect love for the imperfect. The Son Jesus left a heavenly throne to become an outcast in a human society. He came and experienced the coldness of humanity, travelling the bus alone.

Many years ago I rode a big yellow bus to school. Every day the bus was full to capacity with screaming, laughing, playing children. Most of us had a ball. In fact the bus ride to school was the most fun part of the school day - fun for everyone except Peggy. Peggy had jet-black hair. The tangles in her hair disguised any shine. Her eyes were brown like chocolate Smarties, sunken into a pale complexion. She smiled with her crooked teeth despite the insults that they hurled at her every day. "Ewe here comes Peggy. You're not sitting with us. Peggy has lice. You stink. You're ugly . . . "

Yes! Peggy would smile and try to make friends but all the children had Peggy labelled as the outcast. Peggy never gave up trying to belong. Every day she would face her peers, the insults and the rejection. Where is Peggy now? I don't know? I pray Peggy is not still riding the lonely school bus. I pray Peggy has found the Lord and Saviour Jesus Christ. He once rode that same lonely bus.

Perhaps Peggy is a leader strong in faith and love. We never really know what impact our words have on people. Our words have the power to build up or destroy. Depending on Peggy's outlook on life, the struggles she faced, her desire to belong, may have changed her perspective and the way she reacts to others. Maybe she became a bitter and angry person who cares for no one or a person with love and compassion who does care for others.

The Bible states very clearly how much God dislikes evil speaking. Evil speaking being words that defame or take away good reputation. It is an attack on a person's character. It is wise to think about the words we speak to others. Our words will either acquit or condemn us. Words accompanied with action are also important. The combination of the two is a prevailment.

The world is full of man-made clichés. Is it possible for people to survive life's struggles believing in man-made clichés? Clichés may help a person refocus negative thought patterns into positive thought patterns. This can help with depressed tendencies. While this may help for a little while, there is little comfort from words alone. Most clichés lack the basic principle of truth. That being "We need Jesus." We cannot get through all of life's ups and downs on the false power generated from fooling others or ourselves. Inner power can come from no other source than the Lord Jesus Christ. To think we can draw from our own inner self is false and is also a great insult to our great and awesome God. The great I am! Who was! Who is! And Who is to come.

The Lonely Ride on the Bus
CHAPTER 19

1. Read 1 John 3:11-24. What example does Jesus Christ teach about love? How are we to love one another?

2. What are the commands God highlights in these verses?

3. What does it mean to those who obey these commands?

A reject is a person or thing considered as unfit or below standard, to put aside or send back, as not to be accepted, practised, believed or chosen. Someone you fail to show due affection or concern for is a form of rejection - to throw back or not want.

4. What do these scripture references teach about rejection? Isaiah 41:9; 53:3; Titus 4:4; 1 Peter 2:4; Luke 10:16; John 3:36.

For further study:

5. Study 1 Kings 19 - "The Israelites have rejected your covenant, broken down your altars, and put your prophets to death with the sword." Here we see God's own people rejecting God, destroying and killing God's prophets. Have you felt like Elijah - weary and scared, overwhelmed by the battle? What does Elijah do?

6. What does God do in response to Elijah's prayer?

7. What did God do to the Israelites, who bowed down to worship Baal?

8. Peggy has something in common with many prophets in the bible. The prophet Elijah, which means, "The Lord is my God," faced much opposition, but showed tremendous courage. What can we learn from Elijah or Peggy, which would help us deal with rejection and please God? Where do you get your strength or courage?

20

A Director's Nightmare
Reality for Jesus

The auditorium was full of people. The walls were bulging at the seams. There was a noise decimal of ninety-nine point nine. Meanwhile all the actors and singers warmed up their voices, prayed and rehearsed their lines. Tension began to mount, nerves began to work overtime as the time drew near to begin the presentation.

All the fussing with the makeup was done. The opening song began. Anxiously, the cast members stampeded up the narrow staircase like a heard of elephants. Some whispered and giggled with excitement. Others frowned while trying to quiet everyone with an overpowering shhhhhh. The smell of bad body odour mixed unpleasantly. Silence filled the auditorium. The lights were dimmed then the music for scene one began. We were all in our places. Down shone the bright spotlight onto our faces melting our makeup. The music opened to begin the presentation. I was wondering if we could possibly duplicate last night's excellent performance? "Sure," I thought. " Wait a minute . . . OH NO!" Who is that sitting in the front rows, the entire front rows? Proud smiles of Mum, Dad, my sisters and brothers, all my nieces, nephews, friends, neighbour and second and third cousins watched with gleaming eyes.

If I left anyone out that is because they were sitting in the second and third rows.

"Ah, Panic!" Memory loss set in. "What is my next line? I knew them off by heart for the last six months. What is it? . I'll improvise."

"Sigh . . . Scene one, made it through. I wonder if they noticed I forgot my lines? I can't go back out there. Ah! After that embarrassing scene, any confidence I had just went through the double pained church windows."

Scene two begins. Lights go down, music starts. Bang, crash - a sixty thousand-ton wall falls over landing on top of a cast member's head.

Scene five started. We had some very crucial lines to say. The audio system took a vacation to the moon, and all that came out were some muffled noises.

The most climatic scene began. The Roman soldiers marched down the isle. Music heightened while the actor playing Jesus carried the cross. I raced down to meet Jesus, just as we rehearsed it.

"They must have done a rewrite and did not tell me." Jesus dropped the barn board cross on my little size two foot. It felt like a mountain fell on it. My acting ability did improve. I am sure I was crying buckets of salted tears after they picked the cross off my foot and continued with the crucifixion scene. I hobbled over to kneel before the cross weeping intensely.

In the next scene of chaos the strobe light flashed on and off while everyone ran in different directions. Similar to a scene from the three stooges, two cast members collided banging their heads. Others fell over each other. Like I said, a scene of chaos.

The play finally came to a close. We took our bows and gave a salvation message to the audience. Throughout the performance we had a few mishaps but survived. The bruised foot, black eyes and bumps on the head healed quickly. Did the bruised egos heal? Well, the jury is still out on that one. All the mistakes were camouflaged quite well. They just loom large in our inward, self-absorbed minds. The audience thought we performed it very well. So well in fact, they gave us a standing ovation. Jesus deserves the real ovation. There was no humour in His realistic death on that cross.

A Director's Nightmare
CHAPTER 20

1. Have you ever had any situations in your life, which seemed very serious at the time? As you reflect back, can you see any humour or God's sense of humour? How did the situation affect your spiritual growth? What did you learn from it?

2. Study Matthew 27:27- 44 and John 19. Write the parts of this chapter, which touch your heart?

3. In your own words, write what the crucifixion of Jesus means to you?

4. How did people respond to Jesus when He was here? How do people of today respond to Jesus? Why?

5. What was different about Jesus death, from the two other men hanging on the cross on either side of Jesus?

6. In the story The Director's Nightmare, the actor is embarrassed, nervous and worried about trivial things, like family watching, remembering lines etc . . . How do you suppose Jesus felt? What do you suppose He was thinking, as He looked down and saw an audience of family and friends watching him being crucified? (John 19:25)

21

Lost in Space
Keep our eyes on God

ぶ⁘ぷ

Have you ever stared in a daze? Some people call it daydreaming or being in deep thought. I caught myself in a deep thought one day while I stared at my watch? I was feeling bored and lazy though I had a list of things I could do. As I watched the seconds tick away one by one until they became one minute. I was literally lost in time. Time ticked away seconds to minutes. Time I would never get back while living on this earth. The pretty piece of jewellery around my skinny wrist was a shinny gold with a touch of black. The face on my watchband seemed to laugh at me as light shone through the living room window onto the gold hands. Tick . . . Tick . . . I then realized that life was passing away while I pondered it.

A question came to my mind. Why do some people have so much spare time to ultimately waste doing nothing productive? What is productivity anyway? Then there are people caught in a time warp of business and schedules. Going so fast and constant they cannot get off the highway of productivity, and have very little gas left in their tanks.

Two different scenarios yet the outcome is the same.

Many times we waste time on meaningless things like: self-fulfilment, self-destruction, self-absorption, or simply put, selfishness. In either of these scenarios, God may be left out of the plan. One does not have time to pray. The other feels too depressed and lonely to pray. When the two scenarios meet you may eventually get a balance by learning from each other. If one can get past the negative energy created from that wall of self-defence. Together take down the fence and construct a scenario that will make both content.

Let us do the B verses D scenario. D is too busy and does not need another thing added to the list of things to do, especially if it may require any extra time or attention. D feels overwhelmed and a little incensed at B's neediness.

B lacks understanding not being able to relate to D's busy schedule of priorities. B begins to feel unimportant and lonely. This takes away any productivity and creates negative thought patterns, which can contribute to feelings of low self-esteem and depression.

Sounds like these two different scenarios need some help or direction. There are many answers in the Holy Bible that address problems or questions people have. A key verse which addresses these scenarios is found in Luke 12:31 and Matthew 6:33. "But seek first his kingdom, and his righteousness, and all these things will be given to you as well."

Whatever makes people strive for sinful things of this world is dangerous, especially when it takes our eyes off Jesus. Allow God to control our lives instead of struggling through life like a lost school of minnows. God can help us find that spiritual, physical and emotional balance needed in our lives to overcome the world. If we can find this balance everyone will be happier. The trials we may have to endure will be more like little drops of dew on some Spring mornings grass. We can all pray for God's perfect balance.

Lost in space
CHAPTER 21

1. We can all probably relate to one or even both scenarios. What do you think is the honest balance? How do we achieve it? What scenario do you lean toward?

2. What does the scripture say about wasting time? Read Ecclesiastes 3:1-8; 5-9;
   1 Corinthians 7:29

3. Romans 13:8-14 gives a lot of good advice to both B and D. What is the good advice? What is the warning?

4. 1 Corinthians 7:29 - 31. What does it mean, "the time is short?" How does the bible tell us we should live?

5. Matthew 6:33. What does the kingdom of God signify? What is His righteousness including?

22

Prevail to Kinship
Letter to a friend

Finding love in rejection

My dear friend:

I write to you again, knowing and understanding the pain of rejection you are feeling at this time. I do not know why the distance between us, has become like a long dusty road? Even through the dust and silence, clear video footage of old memories flash through my head. They remind me of all the wonderful, precious moments we shared: laughing, praying, encouraging each other the way best friends do.

I send you this book praying that it will comfort and encourage you. May it be an instrument used by our Lord to bring healing to your wounds?

This morning I wiped the glue from my eyes caused from the tears of last night's prayers. God greeted me this morning with a light blue sky, soft and mellow, enhanced by the bright sun. The sun warmed my face. A song of love poured through my window like a thousand angels singing joyfully. The gentle little birds chirped melodically to start my day. Invigorating freshness of all the different blends of Spring's bouquet floated toward me covering me like a delicate veil.

God's blessings are abundant. We often take them for granted. This morning I received all God's beautiful displays of affection, love and friendship.

Again my Saviour and I would meet, talk and listen to one another in the serene solitude of my temporal home. Surrounded by beauty, God's love, I praised my Saviour Jesus. With limited understanding I'm not fully able to comprehend the depth of God's love.

While I was praying, an old seed of rejection swelled within my heart. It felt like a giant air bubble. I believe this helps me to sympathize a little better with the rejection you are dealing with at this time. Pain and rejection have been around since the beginning of creation. Jesus also endured rejection by those He loves, for those He loves. Perhaps it is because we see so much rejection in our day-to-day lives, it becomes an acceptable way of life. We always see rejection in human relationships. Parents reject their children because they do not meet up to their expectations. Brothers reject brothers because of blame and pride. Husbands and wives reject each other because they cannot reconcile differences or they think they have fallen out of love. Friends reject friends sometimes for what may seem no reason at all. The reason for rejection is insignificant. However, the result is a hammer of destruction. I pray you find understanding and a remedy to take away your pain and sorrow. I will share a little advice someone once gave to me. It is a thought bubble to ponder: "Humble yourself under His mighty hand as to take part in great exaltation. Those who allow themselves to be emptied, who patiently suffer rejection and misunderstanding will soon stir the entire world with the King's Message." (Ref. 1 Peter 5:6-1) It may not ease your hurt at this time, but it gives hope for the future.

The joy of the Lord is your strength. So seek joy, and strength will follow. This morning I travailed as I prayed to Jesus, asking him to heal your broken heart. The why questions started to arise. Then He reminded me to trust in Him. Hold onto faith and watch it grow. Hold onto hope. Watch God's promises unfold. God's love flows like an endless stream of living water, always changing, creating growth and fresh water.

I realized the pain and rejection I have caused my Saviour. It is a parallel of rejection that goes side by side. I like to believe that every tear we cry, God cries too. Every hurt we feel, God feels too. Sufferings, we endure, Jesus also injured. Salted tears we cry blend with the tears of our Holy Father's. Our great teacher teaches a lesson of love for all time. The word relationship receives a new meaning. The dictionary describes relationship as what one person or thing relates to another. A kind of connection or correspondence, contrast or feeling that prevails between persons and things (kinship). The key words in relationship are the words: prevail and kinship. (Kinship derived from the word kind). Christ Jesus prevailed over death victoriously when He arose from the grave. He chose to do this for every **kind** of relationship. For God is in control of all things, and He is above all. Jesus exemplifies the love and respect of kinship shown to one another in all relationships. Now I just have to learn to apply Christ's example to my daily relationships.

My friend, I will continue to keep you in my prayers. I pray God strengthens you in every spiritual growth, during your time of sorrow. Sincerely, I pray for a greater understanding of the love God has for you.

I assume you feel a little like Job or similar to someone who has been robbed and left to die. At times that is how rejection has made me feel. My friend I will not leave nor forsake you like all the others who walked by you, ignoring your anguish. You have had enough rejection in your life.

The sight of a wounded bird or an orphaned animal saddens my heart. Knowing the hurt you are feeling saddens me greatly. It perplexes me to think of those you love walking on by you, as if they didn't care about you. My heart breaks for the lack of compassion shown to you and your circumstance. But, we must not judge others, but rather try our best to help clear the dust from the dry, dusty road.

We must continue to love those who have rejected us, even if it hurts to the depth of our souls. In this process we will become more like Jesus, who has demonstrated again and again the true meaning of unconditional love.

Someday the road you travel will consist of gold refined to perfection. Together we will walk the road of life with our Lord Jesus Christ. Until then we must remember that while we are in that valley of despair, we are not alone. Our heavenly Father is with us every step of the way. He says to us - "Do not be sad, my child. I love you and I always will." His kisses heal the wounds of our heart and of our mind. The scars of yesterday bring hope for tomorrow. God loves you and so do I. May our friendship to one another, be the representation of God's love.

I will see you soon.
In Christ's love,

Your forever friend

Prevail to Kinship
CHAPTER 22

1. At some point in your life you may have experienced the rejection from a family member or a close friend. How did this make you feel? How did you cope with these feelings? What was Jesus response to the rejection he endured, when his friends deserted him? Luke 23:34, John 21:15-20.

2. Find a balance in your life, with God, family and friends. Pray and ask God if there are any idols or unbalance in your life, then make a pyramid diagram and write in the order of priority by writing down the names of the people in your life. Try to achieve a balance.

3. An idol can be a material thing or an attitude of the heart. If you are out of balance in an area of your life, check to see if there are any idols. What does God teach us about idolatry? Read Leviticus. 19:4, 26:1, 26:30, Deuteronomy. 32:21, Psalm 106:36, 115:4, Ezekiel. 14:3, 14:4, 1 Corinthians 6:9, 8:4, 10:14, 6:16, Colossians. 3:5, 1 John 5:21.

4. Kindness is a form of hospitality, a friendly attitude toward others. When put into action one can hope to receive the gift of kindness returned. The fruit of the Spirit is very nutritious. What can you do for a friend this week, which will encourage them and make them feel like they are wanted, appreciated and loved?

5. Read John 15:13 and memorize this verse.

6. Read Gal. 5:16-26 and write down the contrast between those who live by the Spirit and those who live contrary to the life of the Spirit.

23

Prevail to Friendship
Letter to a friend

**"Carry each other's burdens, and so
Fulfill the law of Christ." Galatians 6:2**

My dear friend:

Sorry to hear your friendship didn't work out. Did your
friend tell you your friendship is over? Did she say? "Hey
pal. It was only for a season." If that is what she said, then
you can probably relate to these common phrases I will
quote? "Sometimes friendship is only for a season." Or "God
has closed the door on our friendship." Or "Our friendship
was never what you thought it was." Or "It is God's will to
end our friendship." This kind of reasoning can be dangerous
and can contribute to the break up of some friendships, which
in fact may not be God's will. We must be careful that we are
not just attaching God's name to it. God should never be used
as our scapegoat. Does this way of thinking make it seem
acceptable to break someone's heart?

I don't agree with this season - reason for ending
relationships. Many authors fill their friendship books

claiming that signs of co-dependency are valid reasons to get out of a friendship. Sometimes a person who has many needs can be diagnosed incorrectly, as someone who is co-dependant. When in reality they are going through a difficult time and just need someone to be understanding and sympathetic toward them. They need a friend. The message often communicated is that a co-dependant friendship is an acceptable reason for a friendship to be discontinued. Who is really qualified to make such a judgement? It seems that this idea offers an easy excuse to end an unwanted friendship.

Most often the reason is really because of lack of verbal communication, understanding or lack of forgiveness. Do we need to believe that life is just one season after another? Could that be the simplicity of it? It is important to examine ourselves as to understand if our reasons and actions scripturally line up. Ask ourselves and ask God questions. See if we are actually caught in the trap of rejection of another? It is so easy to accept that season - reason philosophy, while hurting someone deeply in the process.

If you are struggling with a broken relationship, answer these questions in relation to your situation. Whom did Jesus ever reject? What would Jesus do? We can't help it if someone close to us dies or moves away. In a case like that, one could possibly say it was for a season and God allowed that to occur. I'm talking about relationships that end for "no particular reason or because someone in the relationship acted up." I just believe that people are so easy to call it quits at the first sign of trouble. Could this be why the divorce rate is so high? Perhaps this is the reason we have so many depressed people in the world? Is this possibly a sad truth to why the suicide rate is rampant? Could this be a reason why teenagers in schools have been shooting their peers? Are these some backlashes of rejection - causing anger, resentment, bitterness, loneliness, malice and all sorts of evil? All of these feelings can leave a snowball effect of one unfruitful reaction of one sin after another. I believe these are also by-products of Satan's direct attack on relationships. Satan is an evil foe; waiting to see whose relationship he can kill, steal or destroy. The majority of this world does not have a Savior relationship with Jesus Christ, yet they must cope with some form of rejection because of someone's easy-come-easy-go attitude. How can they cope?

Early one morning I began to observe the seasons. I was experiencing the changing of seasons from Summer to Fall. At that time, one of my closest friendships seemed to be coming to an end. If we had accepted the season reason for that friendship, our friendship would probably be history now. Our friendship is one of the best friendships I have today. We overcame our differences by seeking to understand each other and accept each other the way we were created. Together we have gone over many bumpy roads. In the process we are learning a lot about humility, loyalty and forgiveness. We are continually finding out the true meaning of friendship, which Christ demonstrated. I like to think we have become true brave hearts to each other. Let's ponder the changes of the seasons in correlation to relationships.

The seeds of Fall bring life in the Spring. Jack Frost begins to make nightly visits marking the land, leaving the grass in a dormant state. When I think of Fall, it brings a sadness with the change. The beautiful garden flowers die off one by one, as the once hot sun distances itself, leaving a cold wind in the air. There are days of contrast, which swiftly nips the linings of our jackets. The sounds of singing birds begin to quiet, as the birds fly south for Winter. Trees are given a new look of bright colorful oranges, yellows and reds. We get to admire one final breathtaking view of God's Fall painting before the trees become leafless stems. The leaves yell out in the cool breeze dancing one more dance.

One by one each leaf falls lazily to the ground. The end of Fall leaves barrenness.

Winter can seem like a long season to endure. It can be a time of barrenness, when the brittle branches even seem less attractive, and grey. God covers the ground and trees with a blanket of whiteness. At times the trees sparkle like diamonds as snowflakes float down from the sky. Winter comes and the snow protects the grass and tulip bulbs, with it's covering, acting as an insulator of warmth over the ground.

Beneath the snow, in the coldness of earth, the swallowed seeds wait in a frozen time zone. As we watch, "time almost seems to stand still." When we look wide-eyed in appreciation, we can endure the winter and find its beauty.

The warmth of Spring comes with the sun. Then the rain washes away the dirt, bringing out the vibrant colours and smells. Before our eyes, everything is restored in the newness of another fresh Spring. Spring is like a symphony of life, an angelic choir, bright, beautiful and reaching heavenward in praise. The same birds return and sing praises into our bedroom windows each morning. The same trees in our back yard grow buds, and leaves, and then they are restored to flourish back to life. Each season is as beautiful as the one before. When summer comes we can sit and admire the garden in our lives. We can praise God for such perfection, appreciating yet another season of life.

Summer is a season of rest; it can be a peaceful representation of God's greatness of all that He is and all that He does. I can imagine God calling each of us, like a Father calls his children. He says, "Come here, look at all these things beautifully created for you."

From one year to the next, I don't find the seasons change all that much, really. Each season brings its times, which we might not particularly enjoy. Overall, each season has more beauty to behold than ugliness. This can make it worth coping through the dull times and the challenges. Whatever the weather of the season, we do change and grow and are fashioned by God to be more like Him. This helps us to better appreciate each season and the people we share it with. As for my friend and me, we look back at our friendship and say wow. We made it through yet another season. We are learning from our mistakes, from our seasons. In the process we are becoming more transparent with each other and with others in our lives.

My friend and I might not necessarily like some of the things we have learned about each other, but we love each other, even with our little quirks. We go on and accept each other just the way God created us. If God can accept us, why shouldn't we accept each other and treat each other the way God teaches us to love? We can all learn how to become brave hearts in our friendships rather than quitters.

May the love of God, get you through your seasons. True love conquers all. When we have Christ leading us through life, there is no season, no mountain too big to get over. If someone has wronged you, forgive him or her. Correct the wrong done. Never let punishment be yours or their reward. Peace, unity, and love from God bring a Spirit of reconciliation. We must learn unfailing love from the Master. How do we achieve that? Follow Christ's example and we might find we get through all the seasons with the same friends. God will get us through. When things are tough, and relationships strained, keep those eyes on Jesus and trust and pray and listen and learn. If your relationships come and go like a season, at least you will have total assurance that it is God in control of your seasons of life - not you. The season - reason will no longer be an easy out or an excuse to reject others. Life's seasons in the natural come and go. They bring life. Each season is new and fresh.

Each season completes a full circle in the cycle of life.

So my dear friend, I pray that you and your friend will overcome your differences. I pray you will both find reconciliation. In the process I hope you both find a close connection of sincere friendship to each other.

In Christ's Love,

Your, forever friend.

Prevail to Friendship
CHAPTER 23

The scripture verses in John 15:9-17, 1 John 2:5 and 1 John 5:2-3, teach the definition of friendship as modelled after Christ.

1. What can we understand about the importance of obedience to God's word? His word will instruct us in how to be victorious over a sinful pattern in our life. What are some truths, which will help us to be victorious daily?

2. How do we show love to God in relation to friendships or other relationships? (1 John 5:1-6.)

3. What does 1 John 5:3 tell us about how to overcome the world?

4. What is the command Jesus gives to His disciples in John 15:12.

5. In John 15:14-17, we learn the rank or privilege to be classified as friends rather than servants. What is the difference? Jesus tells us clearly the definition of a true friend. What is that definition? Jesus also shows the vulnerable characteristic of taking His friends into his confidence, telling everything. What is the fullness of this statement in John 15:13?

6. Again in John 15, Jesus tells us his command to Love each other. We are to obey this command. What does Jesus portray love to be?

7. For further study about love. What is the Biblical definition of what love is and what it is not? Mt 5:44, John 13:34-35, Romans. 12:18 - 20, Romans 13:10, 1 Corinthians 1:7, 3:2
1 Corinthians 3:1-3, 1 John 4:16.

Expressions of love:
Mt. 5:44 - praying for others
John. 13:34-35 - love others the way Jesus loves
Rom. 12:18 - live at peace
Rom. 13:9-10 - Love is the fulfilment of the law.
- Neighbour is anyone who is in need.
1 Corinthians. Chapter 13 - faith, hope and love. The greatest of these is love.

24

Going Home

❧

"In my Father's house are many rooms;"
John 14:1- 4

This is a true story of a happy ending to a person's life. She had her days on the mountaintop and spent some days in the valley. Some might consider her just an ordinary person. I'll share with you the happy ending, which began with a dismal diagnosis.

My family and I had known Marg and her family since I was a little girl. Marg and my Mum were very close friends. We spent many summers together when they stayed in one of our cabins, which were situated in our back yard. Many times I also stayed at Marg and her husband Curly's home. They always made me feel like a daughter. Their children Billy and Tommy were my best buddies. I remember a lot of laughter, card games and corn-roasts, precious memories I can always carry with me. I can enjoy again and again all the great times we shared, as we reminisce.

The last two weeks of Marg's life, I was blessed to get to know Marg in a very special way - In a way that I had never known her all those years. God has a way of breaking down all the barriers of communication, fear, self-centeredness etc.

Love is bigger than fear. Talking is more important than denial. Other people are more important than self. The temporal becomes eternal.

Marg knew that she was going to die. Even in the seriousness of her physical condition, she managed to make me laugh. I discovered an amazing sense of humour and an extremely courageous, caring woman, waiting to move on to eternal life. I was privileged to share in her suffering, while talking intimately with her about life and death. I asked Marg if I could pray for her. You see up until that day, I had no idea what Marg believed spiritually. Life has a way of skipping over spiritual matters and other important issues, like a pebble bouncing over rough water. When you have to face the reality of death, suddenly you have to deal with what comes after death. Marg's concern was not about herself, but for the loved ones she would leave behind.

One Sunday morning I went to visit Marg in the hospital. I told her I was bringing church to her. She thought that was great. We read from the Bible the 23, 24, and 25th Psalms along with other scriptures. We talked about knowing God personally. Marg asked Jesus to forgive her sins and to be her Lord and Saviour of her life. That Sunday morning Marg's name was written in the book of life. Through the next couple of weeks Marg would persevere through the process of her illness and death. The peace of God would be her company until her last breath.

As time passed by, Marg's physical condition increasingly weakened. She lay in her hospital bed. Coherent enough to realize I was by her side. She clasped my hand with a deathly grip. Her eyes could not open. It caused her more pain. With her liver critically damaged and other bodily functions shutting down, she moaned and cried out to God to take her home. With each retching pain her grip was knuckle white. I sat helplessly. I could not take away her pain. Marg fluttered sporadic breaths between moans.

Gently, I caressed her forehead to give her some comfort, then feathered her swollen stomach, while I prayed. All I could do was encourage Marg to call out to Jesus. "Oh Jesus, help me," she moaned, as tears rolled from her closed eyes down to her ears.

It is a strange feeling to be with someone who is dying. I thought for sure God was taking Marg home that day, as her tired body drifted off into a sleep.

Two weeks later, a small group of friends and family would gather around her grave. The summer sun shone bright. Big fluffy, white rabbits filled the sky. A refreshing breeze seemed to bring a comforting arm of peace to our goodbyes. Here we gathered to say our goodbyes to a wonderful wife, mother, sister, grandmother and friend. Marg filled all of these titles to many people.

For myself this was a very different funeral to attend. I have been to my share of sad funerals. One of those funerals was Marg's son Tommy. His funeral was a few years earlier. One summer day, Tommy's body was found lying amongst the grass, below the Bloor Viaduct. Marg laughed as she joked, "When I get to heaven I will be able to chase that Tommy and kick his butt." A smile embellished her face.

Marg's funeral was different because God had allowed me to be a part of Marg's going home. Marg's son Billy asked if I would prepare a eulogy at the gravesite. This gave me an opportunity to share with the family the happiness and peace I believe Marg had about going home to be with the Lord.

There we stood to place her urn of ashes into the ground. As I spoke, we remembered from the first book of the Bible Genesis 2:7 " The Lord God formed man from the dust of the ground and breathed into his nostrils the breath of life, and man became a living being."

Ecclesiastes 3:20: "All go to the same place; all come from dust, and to dust all return." In the Book of Revelation 21:27, which is in the last book of the Holy Bible, we are told of the revelation about our destiny for those names who are written in the Book of Life.

We also have a promise from God as to the place He is preparing for those who believe in Christ Jesus as Lord - a place of many mansions. Marg believed and we believe that Marg is now with the Lord Jesus. She told me, her favourite song was, "I saw the Light." I believe that to be true for Marg. He opened up her eyes she saw the light. No more darkness, no more strife. I believe Marg will be singing this song and many more praises through eternity. Could that be a song for you to sing? In Marg's death, she was born into eternal life.

It is like a baby who lives comfortably in the mother's womb for nine months. The baby is very happy and content to stay there and grow and exist. The time arrives for the baby to leave that nice warm place. The only life that baby has known for nine months. Suddenly a big light shines in the baby's face as it is brought into a new life. The baby goes into a foreign world of life it is not so sure it wants any part of. Afraid of the unknown, the baby fights it all the way. The baby has no choice, but to be born.

Death is a paradox to life. Born into a spiritual life with the Lord Jesus Christ, for all eternity. Without the Saviour Christ Jesus, death becomes an eternal death and a separation from God. No paradox, no life, no peace, no joy or happiness, but eternal death, otherwise known as hell. What song will you sing on that day of judgement, when you stand before the Lord our God?

In Memory of Marg Lemay

Going Home
CHAPTER 24

"In my house are many mansions"

1. Read Ecclesiastes. 7:1-2. Why does a Christian have ample reason to say this?

2. Study 2 Corinthians 5:1-10, and Philippians 1:21-23. The tent is a temporary and flimsy home and wears out over time. (2 Corinthians. 5: 1-6) What does the earthly tent symbolize?

3. What is the difference between an earthly tent and a building from God?

4. What do you think Paul means in 2 Corinthians. 5:4, when he says "so that what is mortal may be swallowed up by life?"

5. 2 Corinthians chapter 5:5-6 teaches us about the Spirit, referring to the Holy Spirit given to us as a guarantee or deposit. What does this mean to you personally?

In the chapter "Going Home," Marg received Jesus Christ as her Savior. She repented and prayed asking Jesus to come into her life. When she prayed, the risen and exalted Saviour applied the benefits of Christ's redemption power over Marg's life.

6. What is Paul trying to convey to us as Christians about life and death in relation to being at home with the Lord as opposed to being at home in the body?

   Justification, redemption is granted to the Christian through faith in Christ as it was for Marg. Each person is accountable for the things we do while in the earthly body or tent.

7. What does 2 Corinthians 5:10 teach us about each person's destiny?

25

My Hero

**"So we fix our eyes not on what is seen,
but on what is unseen.
For what is seen is temporary,
but what is unseen is eternal."
2 Corinthians 4:18**

Is it a plane? Is it a bird? No, it is super . . . The Hero's? Our eyes flood with tears as we watch our fathers and grandfathers march gallantly down a main street for the Remembrance Day parade. We stand heads bowed, tissue in hand as we pause for one minute of silence. We remember the heroes, who died in the wars. A moment to reflect on the sacrifices made, the brutal casualties of war as one cross after another marks the solemn graves. To visit the gravesite we can almost hear the gunfire, the agonizing screams and see the pale death stare of many soldiers. We see the same empty stare in some of the veterans who survived the war, but still relive the war in their memories day after day.

There are some of us who have never had to live out an intense scenario like war. So, we often create make-believe heroes. Whether they are mere cartoons or living people, they are someone we look up to as special. In fact, I can remember, as a young adolescent having a television hero. It was a series called "The Bionic Woman." Every episode

Jamie Summers (the bionic woman) single-handed, saved the world from destruction.

She fought off the bad people and even died and came back to life. So what if she was eighty percent bionic? She could run eighty miles an hour and look as graceful as a swan in flight. Her hair never even got out of place. Jamie was a tennis pro, a school teacher and her boyfriend was the six million dollar man. Who can top that? Was she a woman of noble character? She had it all, so it would appear. Why is there such a need, in society to have a super hero? Are heroes a measuring stick we think we need to measure up to?

I also had a real life hero. Susan was her name. We called her Sue. She didn't run very fast and she was not a tennis pro or a school teacher. The thing that made Sue a hero was that she liked me. My hero made time for me, little me. Sue was older than I, more like an older sister or friend. She let me hang around, while we did fun things like swimming and games. Sue was married to my brother Larry. She would be at our house all the time. I was like her shadow. If she sat in the armchair, I would be sitting on the arm of the chair. I'd sit on the bed and watch as she changed the diapers of Crystal, her newborn baby girl. I was always talking, always very helpful to her of course. My friends had moved away near the same time my sister married and also moved away. Sue filled a void in my life. She became one of my favourite people. Sue was my hero.

However, my hero was vincible. Though she never saved the world, she did have that hero's instinct. One night, when Sue was walking home from work, she decided not to walk all the way to the stoplight. Usually she would cross at the lights. Something was different about this night. Maybe she was in a hurry to get home? Anyway the road seemed clear, not too much traffic. Sue was pushing her little eleven-month-old baby girl in the carriage and her cousin was standing by her side. A couple hundred yards from the light, they stepped off the curb.

Suddenly, a speeding car came out from a side street. In a split second decision, Sue tried to protect her baby by pulling the carriage back. The car still hit the carriage in such a way that it was pushed into the curb. The carriage was crushed. The force of the impact pulled Sue directly into the path of the car. Time stood still as Sue's body went flying up over the hood of the car, sending her air born then to the ground. December 16, 1970 Susan "my hero" was dead. Crystal survived without a scratch and Sue's cousin was not hurt at all.

Christmas was six days after her funeral. I remember opening the gift she had bought me. It was a 10-karat gold ring with the initials BW engraved on it. Christmas morning I opened the nicely wrapped box, which said, "To Becky love Sue." I cherished that ring all through my growing years. When one finger outgrew it, I wore it on my smaller finger. Years later I would marry and I still wore that ring like it was part of my finger. While I was on my honeymoon, I was washing some mud off of my hand by running my hands through the ocean waves. The waves pulled the ring off my finger out into the vast ocean and it was gone. I realized my initials were no longer BW but BH. In a strange way I thought it was time to move on with my life. Time to say goodbye to Sue. Not that I would ever forget Sue, but that it was time to say goodbye.

When Sue died I was a nine-year-old child and I found it very hard to understand why God would take away my hero. Sue's smile is something I will never forget. Her life ended so young. She did not win any prestigious gold metals. Her trophies were few. Some people never had the pleasure of getting to know her. Sue did win one thing. She won a special place in my heart. How did she do that? Simply by making time for others, for making time for me and making me feel special.

Can any good come out of her death? Maybe it could be the hero's seed of love that she planted in all the hearts of those she knew and loved. May her hero's seed grow in us. Maybe we can make someone feel accepted and loved today?

When my hero died, a part of me died too. An empty void remained in my heart, for many years. Then I found Jesus. For many years, I longed to replace the pain and sadness, with one hero after another.

Our human heroes do not last forever. We live in a temporal world. Each temporal day ends as the sunsets, only to rise again to an eternal day. I have learned that we must think and live eternal. By thinking eternal we can make a difference in someone's life. To achieve eternal values, one must look to the eternal provider, which is God Himself. Jesus Christ is the only hero, who really did save the whole world from death. He is our hero's measuring stick. He is a hero that is here eternally whether the sun rises or the sunsets. I'm thankful for my hero. I'm also thankful for the little heroes like Sue, who God puts in our lives. I'm thankful for the special people who touch our lives in a meaningful way. Do you need an eternal hero? Who is your measuring stick? Does your hero fill the empty air pockets in your heart? Let Jesus be your hero.

In memory of Susan Wills
July 20, 1950 - Dec 16, 1970

My Hero
CHAPTER 25

For centuries heroes have lived and died. The Oxford dictionary defines a hero as one of superhuman qualities, favored by the gods, an illustrious warrior. A person admired for achievements and noble qualities.

1. Who are some biblical characters that may have been considered heroes and what heroic act did they do? (See - Acts 6:8 - chapter 7, first Christian Martyr) Luke 11:51, Hebrews 11:23-40). What was it that compelled these characters?

   The biblical version of a hero is a martyr. A martyr is one who undergoes a penalty of death for persistence in Christian faith or obedience to the law of the Church, or undergoes death or suffering for any great cause. A martyr is a constant sufferer for a cause.

2. In Philippians. 3:10. What is it that Paul speaks of experiencing by being martyred for the cause of Christ? Read any footnotes.

3. Study Revelation 6:9-12. What is the vision for those who have been slain because of the word of God?

4. Study footnotes to find out what is the symbolization of blood, (Ex 29:12, Lev 4:7) also the symbolization of the white robe? (See Revelation. 3:1-5,18; 4:4; 7:9,13,14; 19:14).

5. Study Phil. 2:1-11. What examples of humility can we learn from Christ in this scripture?

6. What selfless characteristics should we model after Christ? (Also read 2 Corinthians. 13:14, and Colossians 3:12).

   For further study read Luke 13:34-35 and Matthew. 23:35. Jesus sums up the history of martyrdom in the Old Testament, which also parallels to Christ's death.

26

Noble Character

❦

"Belonging to the nobility; of lofty character or ideals; showing greatness of character, magnanimous, morally elevated; splendid, magnificent, stately, imposing, impressive in appearance; excellent, admirable. Hero - person of superhuman qualities, person admired for achievements and noble qualities."

Did you ever notice that on the days when you have a full schedule of things to do, time seems to scurry by? Have you wondered how you will get everything done? Do you have days when you feel unproductive? Sometimes we believe that being productive means to have long lists of things to do every day. At the end of the day we can look at our checklist and say, "Look at all I did today." It can make one feel good, or build self-esteem and self-worth. It can give one a sense of accomplishment and purpose. One day a friend was telling me all she had done that day, and all the things she still had to prepare. At this time, it was just mid afternoon. She said, "I feel like sitting down and taking a break, but I have too much to do." I think her phone call to me was the only break she had that day. Her list was as long as my arm, cooking, cleaning, laundry, preparing for women's ministry meetings, outreach banquets, an anniversary party and she still wanted to take time to bake for the family and more. I was exhausted at hearing all she did get done, and at what she still wanted to get done that day. I thought wow; you seem to be such a woman of noble character.

My friend reminds me of the story in the bible about the woman of noble character. Proverbs 31:10-31 describes a wife of noble character. The woman of noble character does so many things. Her day is full from early morning until late at night.

My friend asked me, "Have you done anything productive today?" I had to say, "NO, I guess not." In comparison to her day, I accomplished very little that day. It was the anniversary of 9/11. It was a day of remembrance of all the lives tragically taken in the attack on the World Trade Center. Early that morning, I had turned on the television and watched one sad life story after another. I sat and wept at each story. I cried with each family as I watched their faces and felt their pain. Housework did not seem a priority to me that day and seemed rather insignificant. Though I tidied up my kitchen and picked up a few things, emailed a few friends. That was all I could seem to muster.

When I thought about that question my friend asked me, I felt bad that I had no involvement in preparing Grande functions for anniversaries or church outreach programs. Those things are all important functions. For a moment, I felt like a lazy housewife, because my house was not perfect. Then I thought about it. I remembered the scripture from Romans 12:15 "Rejoice with those who rejoice; mourn with those who mourn." Ecclesiastics 3:1. "There is a time for everything, and a season for every activity under heaven": Ecclesiastic 3:4 "a time to weep and a time to laugh, a time to mourn and a time to dance." There is also a time to do housework. The Lord does not like us to live idle lives. However, there are times to be still - times when God wants to touch our hearts through the lives of other people and vice versa.

Perhaps I did just what God wanted me to do that day. On that Remembrance Day, many strangers, of none I have ever known, touched my heart. Their pain, sadness, grief was written all over their faces and their hearts. I cried with them, feeling like I was part of their family. In some small way I could relate to how they were feeling. Life does have its twists and turns. We never know where the road leads. For those who believe in Jesus Christ, the road leads to heaven. Each life is a road. Many roads go right through our hearts. Some roads are straight, and some are bumpy or smooth. Others have sharp turns and steep grades. All are roads. Just like a road that goes through a mountain, each new road leaves an opening for God's light to shine into that heart of darkness. For the true-life stories of the survivors of 9/11, many roads pierced through my heart that day. Now I think that yes, what I did was productive, but in a different way. I did nothing of noble character that day. Perhaps I was keeping my best friend Jesus' company. I believe we both sat on that couch and wept at the hurt of all those families. I seemed to sense His Holy presence. We sympathize with the mothers who lost their sons or daughters - children who lost their parents - others who lost their brothers or sisters or best friends. They are all deep hurts. They are the stories of heroes. Lives sacrificed for others - lives of noble character. There was one of many stories, which touched my heart. The story was echoed through a Father and his love for his son: With a small tear in this Father's eye, his lip quivered as he tried to hold back the tears. This Father told the story of his son and of a little red bandana that he gave to his son when he was a young boy. The Father told his son to always keep that bandana in his pocket. It would always be useful.

The young boy who respected his Father did just what his dad had told him to do. He carried that red bandana in his back pocket everyday right up to the day of September 11, 2001. On that day, this Father's son was in one of the Trade Center Towers. When the tower was hit, the rooms burned with melting heat. Billowing black smoke poured out of the windows. This young man put the red bandana around his face to protect himself. He was an unknown hero. He heard the cry of a woman call for help. Instead of ignoring the woman's cry and saving his own life, he pulled the woman down the stairs to safety. He then went back up the stairs to help more people who were wounded. He saved a few lives. One of the women he saved said that she only knew him by the red bandana wrapped around his face. One more time he went into help others, but it was too late. The Father was proud of his son and what he did. But knowing about his son's heroism does not take away the pain and sadness he feels nor does it remove the empty void that is now in his heart. I imagine he would like nothing more than to have his son back and do all the things he and his son used to do together. I'm sure as he glances at that picture of his son as a young boy, wearing that red bandana; he is reminded of his heroic son. When he does, he feels that great loss again and again.

I'm reminded of another scripture from John 15:13. "Greater love has no one than this, that he lay down his life for his friends." This young man is admired and remembered for his nobility and Christ-like qualities. It is rare that someone would lay down his or her life for a friend. This unknown hero laid his life down for strangers. This was one story of many heroes. They will all be missed but not forgotten.

Noble Character
CHAPTER 26

1. In Ruth 3:11 Boaz tells Ruth "All my fellow townsmen know that you are a woman of noble character." Read Ruth chapters 1,2,3. What is the evidence of her noble character?

2. Proverbs 31:10-31 and give examples of noble character. What are some of the things this woman does throughout her life, which would be noble?

3. In the Parable of the Sower in Luke 8:15. What does the seed in good soil represent?

4. a) Read Philippians 4:1-9. In Paul's exhortations, he tells us to think about such things. What are some of the things we are to think on, which would go hand in hand with being noble?

   b) Which of these things can we do to bring about peace?

5. In 2 Timothy 2:20-22, we read about the contrast between being noble and ignoble. What would characterize ignoble behavior?

6. When we cleanse ourselves from the ignoble, how will that change our lives?

7. For further reading Ecclesiastes 3. "A Time for Everything."

8. Is there someone in your life who has shown noble character toward you? What did they do? What can you do to be noble?

27

The Empty Bed

❧

**"Peace I leave with you; my peace I give you.
I do not give to you as the world gives.
Do not let your hearts be troubled
and do not be afraid."
John 14:27**

It was one of those hot summer days when you could just lounge around in the swimming pool, and sip ice tea with a couple of close friends. At times there is a drawing of the Spirit to leave that place of bliss and comfort. It is a time to fulfill some divine appointment that God has laid upon our hearts. This day would be another lesson in humility. I call it lesson seventy-seven. It is just one of the infinite number of lessons to be learned.

One day our visitation team from church went to make a visit to an elderly man who lived at Rest Haven, a home for the elderly. We had heard that he was not feeling well emotionally and physically. We went on our mission, which was to bring him some fellowship and to discuss with him about eternal life. When we arrived, there was Fred lying in his bed with his head elevated and the limb of his bandaged leg resting on the top of his covers. We introduced ourselves and gave him a flower to brighten up his room. He said he was not feeling very well that day. Fred was gracious and kind and seemed very happy to have three lovely ladies sit at his bedside. We chatted for a while and he told us many stories of his youth, and the journey of his eighty-two years of life.

Fred told us all about being a combat pilot in the Air Force during World War II. He shared how horrible it was and about the many atrocities he witnessed during that time. He said, "Many of the things I saw and experienced are really too terrible to speak about." He said, "It was strange to be in gun fights, with the bullets being fired at me and having to shoot back at them." He shared how his plane was shot down and how he parachuted from the plane and survived. Many of his mates did not survive being shot down. When the war was over, Fred went to University and later worked for many years in the sciences. In the later part of his life he farmed a couple hundred acres of farmland at Mount Forest. As he told the stories, we could almost imagine him as he was then, a two hundred and forty-pound man about six foot two. But here on this day he was not much more than 110 lbs.

Fred told us a story of when his mother had died. He said after his mother died, he heard a knock at the door. As he opened the door, he saw this little white snow owl sitting on the door knob. He took it as a sign that his mother was at peace. So, as Fred shared his delightful stories with us, we found ourselves drawn into who this man was. We talked about life and death. We talked for a long time about being able to have the assurance of eternal life. Fred listened as we shared. Then we prayed a prayer together and Fred confessed his faith. Many times during our visit, he thanked us for coming and hoped that we would visit again.

I remember that first day of our visit - the walk down that long dim hallway. It seemed so long and almost like it was closing in on me. You see I hadn't visited an old age home since my Dad had passed away almost two years earlier. As I walked down the hall to Fred's room, my eyes welled with tears.

I had to fight back the tears with a dry lump in my throat. I remember walking into his room and seeing this replica of my Dad lying in that bed. My memories of my dad were mixed with visions of him sitting there as Fred was, but also the vision of my Dad's lifeless body the last time I sat at his bedside alone. I couldn't believe all this emotion that was trying to pour out of me. I had to try hard to keep it inside. After all, here I was, our purpose was to minister to Fred. When we left Fred that day, I left with all those emotions. A few days later, I experienced some grief as inner healing was taking place. For the first time since my Dad's death I began to grieve my loss. We all grieve our losses in our own time and in our own way. Seeing Fred ignited a spark of healing in my grief.

A week later Alison and I would go back to visit our new friend Fred. I took my guitar because I had promised Fred I would come back and sing him a song. When we arrived, Fred was up in the lunchroom with all the other patients. So, up to the lunchroom we went. Fred and all his companions were sitting in wheelchairs at their lunch tables. Fred was still not eating any food. We took him a couple of chocolate bars and some cans of pop. It may not have been that nutritious, but that is what my Dad loved to eat, so I thought Fred might like to eat them too. With sweaty palms I sang to Fred a couple of songs. He enjoyed the music. Fred thanked me again and again for singing for him.

Again we would talk and talk about many things. That was something I never did with my own dad. In my visits with my dad the conversations were one-sided. He never said a word or responded when I told him I loved him. With some difficulty, he could have, but he just never did. Ironically, I thought I was ministering to Fred. God was really doing something different. He was using Fred to minister to me.

We left Fred that day and he said and did something that I always desired to hear from my own Dad. Even though I have realized that my Dad loved me in his own way, he just never knew how to express his love to me verbally.

Fred took my hand as I reached out to shake his hand and say good-bye. He gripped it as tight as he could. With his bruised skinny arm and big hand Fred pulled me close and kissed me on the cheek, then he spoke the words of a Father when he said, "I Love You." In my surprise, but with a genuine God planted love in my heart I replied, "I love you too." His words touched my heart so much; I cried all the way home. It meant so much to hear those words from Fred. He was my messenger angel. Before we left, Fred asked if we would come back and visit again. We said, "Sure we would come back."

In the reality of life, time did not stand still for a second. The next week and the busyness of life prevented a visit. I wanted to go back and spend time with Fred again. I had ideas of helping him get a prosthetic leg, so he could walk again. Though I thought of him often throughout the week and prayed for him, I regret not finding the time to visit him.

The following week I went to visit Fred by myself. I walked down that long hall to Fred's room. I could see all the wheelchairs lining up to take the elevator up for dinner as I walked. Then I looked in Fred's room to see him. Time stood still. There was the empty bed. It had a colourful blue and pink embroidered quilt covering the bed. The walls were grey and empty except the pin holes which once held up all of Fred's old calendars of dogs. He liked dogs. The cluttered corner where he kept his few belongings was empty. The flowers were gone. In the silence of the empty room, I knew that Fred was gone too. For a moment, I felt sadness in my heart. I learned from the nurse that Fred had passed away the previous week, not long after our last visit.

It is a strange feeling and a wonder to me how we can become so attached to others, to strangers within such a short time? God uses moments such as these in many different ways. Impact moments can bring healing, a loving touch or a kind word spoken. Impact moments can change a frown into a smile, even if it is for a brief moment in time. Why? Moments like these make a difference. Fred may have had many reasons to be sad and depressed. He never showed it.

In those brief visits, Fred had shared so much of himself with us. I think what impacted me most was the love he shared and gave to me. The nurse said that Fred had not been happy for some time. They had amputated Fred's leg. He had no family and lost some dignity. This caused depression and he had stopped eating. I believe that Fred is sitting at a banqueting table now with Jesus. Fred had an assurance of eternal life and a peace about dying - a peace which passes all human understanding. My lesson seventy-seven: Don't put off until tomorrow what you can do today. Don't let the impact moment slip away. You never know what impact you might make in someone's life or how they may impact you. Good-bye Fred. It was nice getting to know you. Thanks for the impact you had on me. Thanks for loving me.

July 20, 2002 - In memory of Fred

The Empty Bed
CHAPTER 27

1. I think the last words Fred spoke to me were the words of a Father - the words: "I love you." Fred barely knew me. God knows me enough to know how much I needed to hear those words. Those three words hold such power and healing in our lives. Read Psalm 136. What are the different situations mentioned and what is the main response to each?

2. I believe God showed me His grace and love, when Fred said the words I had always desired to hear.

   a. Can you think of a time when someone spoke the words you needed to hear at that exact moment you needed to hear them? What response did you have emotionally? How did those words make you feel?

   b. What response did you have verbally to the person who spoke those words to you? What reaction did you have toward God? Did those words change your perspective on anything?

3. Meeting Fred was a divine appointment. Definitely impact moments for both of us. What is the biggest impact someone has had on your life or that you have had on someone else's life?

4. The 23rd verse of Psalm 136, "To the One who remembered me in our low estate, His love endures forever." Fred was feeling in low estate, depressed, lonely and physically not well. Yet the love of God was all that we could see coming from him, a man who was soon to die. Say a prayer of praise to God, whose love endures forever.

28

Pennies From Heaven

❧

Twelve pennies can buy one bag of beans for a hungry child.

Do pennies ever fall from Heaven? Often we walk to our destination, whether it is to work, school, or home. Our head and eyes are looking down. There on the ground may be a nice shiny penny. Sometimes we see a penny that bears the test of time. It is worn down, scorned from years of being tread upon by rushing cars and stepped on by people in a hurry. The penny may have even been noticed, but still left there to sit on that roadside. Who could bother using energy or time to stop and pick up a penny? Some have too much pride to be seen picking up a penny. These days, one penny by itself cannot buy much of anything. Some might dare to look around and make sure no one is looking and quickly bend over and pick up the penny and put it into their pocket. I wonder if the poor, homeless people who are living on our city streets would pick up that penny? So, I ask again, do these pennies fall from heaven? If they do, does God sit and watch those of us who live in wealthy countries, as we walk by these "pennies from heaven" day after day?

Does God watch simultaneously those in the world who live in hunger, barely clothed - those who would appreciate so much what one or two pennies could provide them in the way of food, shelter, medicine or clothing?

What does God think? Does He weep for His children, for those who are in need? The Bible says in Matthew 25:35 & 36 "For I was hungry, and you gave me something to eat, I was thirsty and you gave me something to drink, I was a stranger and you invited me in, I needed clothes and you clothed me, I was sick and you looked after me, I was in prison and you came to visit me." We as Christians wear the name of Christ Jesus. Do we bring honour to His name? Are we fulfilling His scripture? Do we respond to people especially those who are in need, in the same way Jesus responded to the crowds? Did Jesus ever allow the red tape of the Pharisees and their laws to interfere with the mission? Did Jesus leave the hungry without food? John 6:5-14. To paraphrase, Jesus saw the multitudes. A young boy had five loaves of bread and two fish. That day, they fed more than 5,000 men and still there was food left over. In human understanding, two fish and five loaves of bread seemed like very little resources. Jesus used the little they had to the fullest potential necessary to feed the hungry. Are we as Christ's church using all of the resources to the same potential or example of Christ Jesus? Or do we fall short of the mark, by leaving the multitude of hungry children on the beaches of Galilee with two fish and five loaves of bread? Some would say that we can only do so much. We can't help everyone. We can't ask others to give too much out of their pocket books. I wonder if the point of the mission gets lost in the red tape and excuses used or because of our own lack of faith in what God can still do today? Is there too much "we" and not enough HIM/GOD? God is a big God. His capability is endless.

In reality, it is not too much to ask of someone, to pick

up a penny and put it in a bottle and label it food for the orphans, the hungry, the poor? After all they are "pennies from heaven" and just maybe God put them there to feed the hungry, in the same way He gave manna - hidden manna from heaven to feed the Israelites, many years ago. Manna was the heavenly food available to the believer.

Is God the same yesterday, today, and tomorrow? The bible says that HE is. Who has to change then? Is it we, who fellowship in our big churches with our big buffets, with our big budgets? Maybe we need to give all control over to the God of the universe? If God can meet the need of those on the beach, or in the desert, He can meet our budgets too. God can multiply the pocket books. Most important, God can take a few pennies and feed the multitude. It all belongs to God anyway.

We as His children can have the awesome privilege to be like Philip, Andrew, Simon and Peter. We can hand out the loaves of bread that the "Pennies from Heaven" can buy. We can choose to be Disciples of Christ Jesus in this present day, available to do whatever God asks us to do.

Instead of putting a lid on the empty water bottles and throwing them in the recycle bin, we can choose to fill them full of "Pennies from Heaven," and let the living water of Christ Jesus still flow today. Today is the day of His salvation. Don't wait for the right time. Time does not stand still. Tomorrow may never come. This is His time and this is our time that God has given to us, to make a difference in the world today. How will you make a difference?

Pennies From Heaven
CHAPTER 28

1. In Matthew chapter 25:14-28, Jesus tells the parable of the talents. What is He teaching us about how we should use the talents we are given?

2. How could this teaching apply to us in regards to pennies from Heaven?

3. Read Matthew 25:35-41. Who was the King referring to when He said "the least of these?"

4. John 6:1-15 tells about the miracle of Jesus feeding the five thousand with five small barley loaves and two small fish. After they were all fed, what did Jesus say to do with the leftovers John 6:12?

5. What will God give to those who have ears to hear what the Spirit has to say and to those who overcome? Revelation 2:17

6. Read Numbers 11:7-10. What was manna and what was the purpose of God sending manna?

7. In what way could we look at pennies as also being like manna? Referring to Revelation 2:7 and Numbers 11:7-10

29

Camping With Teenagers
God created all things

I f you are a camper, then you might relate to this story. I'm sure you have stories just like this one. If you have teenagers and have gone camping you might even get a laugh out of our story. My two teenagers Kyle, Maegan and myself went on vacation with my friend Dianne and her two sons Jason and Curtis. Every year we go on our annual week away camping with our children. Our children are growing up so fast. We could not believe that this was our ninth summer of camping together.

We set up camp on an Indian campground called Cape Croaker. It seemed like an empty camp ground as compared to the over booked and full Provincial and National Parks. It is amazing how natural the environment is at Cape Croaker. Tall Maple trees cover the peninsula like a carpet of green. There are miles and miles of breathtaking hiking trails, which take you along picturesque lookouts. The lookouts take your eyes to fields of farmland, trees and a body of water, which is the most beautiful shade of blue. My legs went rubbery many times on our hike, as the brave and fearless teens were not satisfied with just looking out and standing back from the edge of this mountain. No, they had to get as close to the edge as possible to look out. Beneath their feet was about a three hundred-foot drop along the edge of the escarpment. They made me very nervous standing so close to the edge, and they knew it. My heart was pounding and I yelled, "Get back!" They replied, "Oh Mom, you are being paranoid."

My idea of camping is sitting around the campfire, writing in my journal. I get great pleasure looking up at the trees and listening to the birds sing. There is enjoyment in listening to the chipmunk's rustle in the leaves as they sneak up to you looking for food or when they eat nuts out of your hand. Watching the maple trees and their leaves dancing with the light breeze brings relaxation, as the wind lightly brushes my face.

But . . . there was not going to be much of this kind of rest for this middle-aged dreamer. Dianne's idea was more like a fifteen-kilometre bike ride up and down rolling hills in the hot sun. Sweat was rolling down my forehead and dripping from my chin. Everyone waited patiently for me at the top of each hill, while I pushed my old bike, feeling that age had crept up to me. I kept thinking, when would I ever get to the top of the hill. We would reach the top of the hill and with great excitement; I would begin to sing a short praise song to the Lord. As I looked to the road ahead, I noticed an even bigger hill to push that bike up. Where was the campground? Where is my chair? A nice cool lake to swim in would be nice. How much farther to go until we get there? Thoughts like these consumed my mind while I grumbled all the way back to the campsite. The ice-cold lake water felt so refreshing when we finally arrived back to the campground and went for a swim.

The next day we took a nine-kilometre hike across the peninsula. Dianne said, "it would take a couple hours." It seemed like eternity, as time stood still. We walked up and down hills going through an endless bush of trees, walking from one side of the escarpment to the other side.

I don't think I have ever felt my age like I did on this camp trip. Neither mind nor body was up to the task. But I did survive and everyone survived my complaining. After a hike like that, all of us were ready for a nice steak cooked on the fire, a cup of campfire coffee, and a rest while those campfire flames pointed toward heaven. It was great, until it began to get dark and some company wanted to join us. Usually racoons are expected. Sure enough a racoon waddled up to say hello. He quickly scurried away when we threw a stone into the grass beside him. Remember this was not your typical campground.

To our surprise another little furry animal came for a visit. It was about eight feet tall with great big giant iron jaws and dinosaur teeth. It had claws the size of Texas and it roared like a Raptor. As I lay in my nice lawn chair by the fire eating my steak and sipping my coffee, it stood over me like it was doing some kind of mating dance. It then reached down and grabbed my steak off of my plate, took my coffee out of my hand and drank deeply, giving a big burp. I screamed and jumped out of my chair only to realize that I had fallen asleep while my steak was burning on the fire grill. We did have some real visitors each night and they were cute little black animals with white stripes down their back. Relatives of Pepe Le Pew. They came at us from all sides. Many nights my fear of being sprayed sent me to bed early. But Maegan and Jason decided to stay up by the fire. It was quite obvious that they liked each other in a new way. They braved the darkness of night and counted seven skunks as they walked into our campsite. The skunks acted like they owned it. The skunks didn't seem to mind that Maegan and Jason were sitting there watching them. In fact they walked under Maegan's chair while she was sitting in it. She didn't move a muscle. After five nights they had given each skunk a name.

The scariest night of all was when we allowed Maegan and Jason to go for a walk. We were all about to go to bed. The teens decided they just wanted to take a walk around the loop. The stars lit up the night, so they didn't take a flashlight. Two hours went by and they were not back. Furious and worried at this point, Dianne and I were wondering where on earth they could be? What were they doing? It was 1:30 in the morning and they were not back. It does not take that long to walk around the loop. You can just imagine all the thoughts that go through a mother's mind. Dianne and I had thought of everything. We drove around the campground, we walked around the campground and called their names and could not find them anywhere. We were about to call in the search and rescue. We prayed that we would find them safe. Finally they walked back to the campsite like there was no care in the world. Needless to say, we had a lot to say to them. It turned out they were sitting on a picnic table a few campsites down from our site, talking about stuff. They saw our van go by, but never thought anything of it. They didn't see the problem. They were grounded to our campsite for the rest of the week. Teenagers! You can't live with them and you can't control their hormones.

We just chalked it up to a few more grey hairs. We praise God that they were safe and that all our worry was for nothing. Despite the little annoyances, which creep up when we are camping, we praise God. For the broken tent zippers, spraying skunks, the red squirrel that made a hole in the camper window invading the peanut bag and spreading peanut shells everywhere, we give thanks.

The racoons raided the dining tent and opened up the cooler and drank all the drinking boxes. They even used the straws. Sure, we had our little frustrations, which annoyed us. Yet we give God Praise that we are given the opportunity to share in such life experiences with close friends.

Experiencing His creation, breathing the fresh air, swimming in the clean fresh water, climbing His rocks and walking His trails, are such blessings given to us to enjoy. It is during moments of camping when we really do wish time would stand still, because the time always goes by so fast. Before we knew it our camp trip was over for another year and we were pulling up the tent pegs, snuffing out the fire for the final time. It almost left a sadness to leave that place of peacefulness. There is a peace when you are camping, even when things are not always the way you may have planned. In our minds we go home and we remember the snapshots of our camping vacation. We smile and laugh as we remember what a great time we really had.

Camping With Teenagers
CHAPTER 29

1. Write your adventurous story of camping or an experience you had which was similar?

2. Did you feel God's presence with you? If yes in what way did you feel His presence?

3. Write a poem about your experience?

4. Read Revelation 4:11. Who created all things? What does God receive?

5. In what way have you ever felt such gratitude toward God while appreciating His creation?

6. How did the elders in John's vision show this gratitude toward God? Read Revelation 4:1-10.

7. What is John's description of God from his vision?

8. What do you think God looks like?

30

More than a Silhouette
God sees all things

This morning I looked out my window. Condensation covered the glass window obstructing my view. The dew lay thick, like a silk blanket upon the grass. It is a good sign that summer is almost over. Another summer has come and is almost gone. The thought brings a little sadness because of things not done. It puts you in that reflective mood. People have a different perspective on life, on their summer. I guess it would depend on what your summer was like, in the things you did or did not do? It is just so obvious that for the most part in life, time does not stand still, although we do experience moments and situations where the clock seems to be stopped.

There are milestones that many of us have to face. For many people having a 30th, 40th, 50th, 60th or 80th birthday can cause some people great anxiety. Maybe it is knowing that the clock is ticking. We begin to examine life more carefully. The things we once took for granted, we now appreciate much more. Things like youthful looks, hair on our heads, health, financial security and friendships. We get to an age and wonder how our children grew up so fast. We begin to look around and notice the generation gaps. Then one day, we realize that we just stepped into the time machine of life and we are now where our mothers and fathers were twenty or thirty years ago. We analyse our lives and we realize that goals we made as youthful teenagers, have still not been achieved. We ask ourselves and we ask God, now what?

We have mulled over the carnage from the years of mistakes and bad decisions. We begin to wonder what happened to those ole school friends? Whatever happened to Joe who was once your so-called best friend? Maybe there have been many Joes and many regrets? Maybe you're at the age where all your friends and many loved ones have passed away one by one? My mother is in her eighties and she has experienced many losses. It was painful to experience the loss of her oldest son and her husband.

It seems that for many people when we reach the age of forty, we begin to wonder about many things. Maybe that is why it is called the wonder years? We wonder, what will people remember about me when I'm gone? Will anyone even notice when I'm not here? Have I impacted anyone's life in a positive way? Have I contributed anything of good to this world? I wonder . . .? It is human nature to believe that we individually have some great purpose to fulfill. When we reach these milestones, sometimes we feel like we are replaceable and have fulfilled no great purpose. At a Sunday morning church service, I noticed this silhouette of a man. He was sitting in the shadows behind the black curtain. I had noticed him sitting there other Sunday mornings fulfilling his function. His legs were crossed and his head was leaning on his hand. As the music played for the offertory and he sat there, I couldn't help but wonder what he was thinking about. Was he praying, talking to God or thinking about the football game? Every Sunday, the quiet person sat behind the church curtain, faithfully giving of his time moving the audio buttons up and down. Are you like the man in the booth? Do you think nobody notices? Are you the man behind the curtain who does not want to be noticed? Maybe you are the nursery worker who takes care of the children so the young mothers can have a break. When it may seem like no one else notices what you do, God notices.

Throughout our lives, we all reach these milestones. For a time our thoughts may be a little clouded with questions, emotions and even feelings of low self-esteem and low self-worth. It is during these times, when time does not stand still, that we must lean on God and His promises. There is a small verse from the bible where God tells us, - "For I know the plans I have for you, declares the Lord, plans to prosper you and not to harm you, plans to give you hope and a future."

Jeremiah 29:11

TIME belongs to God who is the Creator of all things. He will do all things in His time. So if you feel a little down at this time in your life, uncertain of what to do today or tomorrow, don't give up your dreams, your goals or your hopes. Keep your head up high and your eyes on Jesus. He has you and the entire universe in His hands. Acknowledge God and He will direct your life.

In the realm of eternity, what really matters, is knowing that Jesus sits with the quiet man behind the curtain in that music booth. He helps the nursery worker hold the little children on their lap. He rocks the chairs of comfort. For those who are at home alone praying for others, Jesus is the cushion beneath the bended knees. Jesus is your Shepherd. He will be your friend and your companion. He is your every need met. He is God. He will carry you home some day. There aren't any clocks in Heaven.

More than a Silhouette
CHAPTER 30

1. Read Jeremiah 29:11. Make a list of your goals, which have not be met yet?

2. What hope and promise is God giving you personally as you read Jeremiah 29:11?

3. As you go about your daily life this week, take notice of people like the man behind the curtain. Send them an encouraging card or tell them that you have noticed more than their silhouette.

4. How do we keep reaching toward our goals? Hebrews 12:1-3.

5. Sometimes we have to work hard to attain these goals. What are some helpful hints mentioned in 1Corinthians 9:24-27, which will help you reach that goal?

6. In all we strive for we need hope to endure. God promises us hope. Read Psalm 131. If you have a particular hope or need, give it over to God by saying your own personal prayer. Put your hope in the Lord both now and forevermore.

31

Square Peg in a Round Hole

We are the Peg - He is the Carpenter

Approximately eight years ago, I was asked to give my testimony. I had just gone through the eleven steps to freedom. I prayed many prayers taken from Neil Anderson's book "The Bondage Breaker." I was feeling such freedom from past sins, a renewed confidence in my faith in Christ. The condemnation I had felt had disappeared. The shame I had carried around for many years no longer plagued my mind, heart and emotions. I felt free. I was quite willing to share the freedom I felt with others, as a testimony to what God can do in someone's life, by putting their trust and faith in Christ Jesus.

Our annual Ladies' Fellowship was planned and I was asked to share my testimony. The timing seemed so perfect. However, it can seem like it does not matter how free one may feel. There is always someone who will say something to you that attacks that freedom. People say things out of concern for your well being without realizing the negative message it conveys. There was a part of my testimony that I was cautioned not to share, for fear that some of the ladies may gossip about me. These fears may have been legitimate. We all know how women love to gossip. However, fear is not something that God gives us. He does not give us a spirit of fear. 2 Timothy 1:7 *"For God did not give us a spirit of timidity, but a spirit of power, of love and of self-discipline."* I thought and prayed about the word of caution that was given and I felt strongly that I should not omit anything from my testimony.

The evening of ladies' fellowship arrived. For the first time I would share openly with the ladies about my life, the struggles and the victories.

That night a young woman named Debbie was starting to attend our church and came to the ladies' fellowship. Over time, Debbie became an active member. To this day she is involved teaching bible study, co-ordinating women's events and helps with a deliverance ministry at that church. One day Debbie told me that when she heard my testimony, she felt that this was a church for her. She felt that there was a freedom and something different about this church. My openness to share honestly and vulnerably spoke to her in a special way. At the time she had previously attended a church where she felt she could not fit in. She said she felt like a square peg in a round hole. It was not long before Debbie was coming out to our bible studies.

In tears, one day Debbie shared with the women in our bible study, about the rejection she had felt from the women at the church where she had been attending. She had deep hurts from not being accepted and welcomed by those women. She said it did not matter what she tried to do, she felt she just did not fit. We prayed with Debbie and welcomed her and showed her love and compassion. Debbie has now found her place at that Baptist Church where she is quite involved in ministries. I marvel at her growth, her leadership and how she teaches women. It is wonderful to see the impact she has on the women at that church where she now attends. Her love for the Lord and genuine care for the women are so evident as she shares Christ with such sincerity, humility and compassion. Unfortunately the beginning of Debbie's story is not a rare occurrence. Fortunately in the end, Debbie did find victory and acceptance.

I find it ironic that where we should find love, acceptance and always feel welcomed into the family of God, this is not always the case. Sadly, sometimes people are made to feel unwelcome, not needed and not chosen.

This may not be the intention, but it can still leave one feeling rejected. We have experienced forgiveness, unconditional love, redemption and most of all acceptance, by the grace shown toward us from an awesome and loving God. Why then is it so hard for the church to consistently model these things to others?

Maybe you are like Debbie. Do you feel like a square peg in a round hole? Maybe you have been at a church for many years and want to be more involved in the church, but you have been told that you cannot be on the team. The teams or committees are formed and they have chosen someone else to be on their team. You feel rejected and it hurts. It seems inconceivable. It is like being in a family and being told that you are not invited to help organize a special event for your Father. Have you felt like a Cinderella? Then you know what I'm talking about.

If you have felt that rejection from your brothers and sisters in the Lord, you are not alone. Christians are not perfect. They are just people - people who still make mistakes and wrong decisions. Christians are children of God. They are still in the learning process that takes a lifetime. In the process, sometimes people can unintentionally get hurt. It can come in many different ways. Maybe you have been made to feel like you don't meet the standards of the church doctrine, committees or whatever teams it is which has rejected you. In your heart you feel that you have the same right as your brother or sister to be there. Have they said to you, "Don't call us we will call you when we need you." It leaves one with a feeling one cannot explain but only experience. Jesus experienced it too. We don't expect it. We don't understand it. It can make us cry. It can make us soft or it can make us hard. Initially it can leave one with a fleeing feeling, to search for some place else to belong. In Debbie's situation the Lord did take her to another church and it is fruitful. On the other hand, sometimes it takes time to develop relationships and time for others to get to know you by communication.

We might want to seek a new family where we can feel needed, wanted, and accepted. But the danger is that we can lose our focus from our original goals and get off track as we start searching all over again. One can easily become a church hopper. It can take us back a few steps; interrupt progress, side step the purposes of seeing others grow in faith. It can keep us going in circles in the same way Moses and the Israelites roamed the desert for many years. Time does not stand still. The devil loves to see us waste time. We hope and pray for a place, somewhere we will be given the freedom to use our abilities God has given to us, to the fullest.

What did Jesus do? We know He never rejected anyone who wanted to follow and serve Him. We know God's own people rejected Him and killed Him on that cross. We know Jesus has and always will welcome anyone into the family of God who sincerely comes to Him. A few years ago, a friend gave me this little poem.

They drew their circle,
And left me out
A rebel, a heretic
A thing to flout.
But Love and I
Had the will to win:
We drew a bigger circle
And drew them in.

Adapted from Edwin Markham's "Outwitted"

This is a message Jesus taught and lived. It is times like these that we must realize that even though we might not fit into the cliques or meet people's standards or qualifications set, even in some of God's churches. We do qualify. We qualify because of God's grace. When we receive Jesus as our Saviour, we may not meet all His standards either because His standards are perfect as He is perfect. We are still accepted into His family. We are a part of the Family of God.

No one else can tell us any differently, and speak the truth. If you have come to that place and feel rejected, there is a scripture that is true. God has given it to me many times when I have had these bridges or rivers to cross.

Joshua Chapter 1:9. "Have I not commanded you? Be strong and courageous. Do not be terrified; do not be discouraged, for the Lord your God will be with you wherever you go." It is not easy at all, but with God's help, we try to pick ourselves up, dust ourselves off and start all over again. God will use each of us in many different ways in the ministry. In reality we don't even need to be on a committee or on that team, though it would be nice.

One day, God ministered to me through a man who was sitting alone at a picnic table. He ministered to my sadness as I opened a letter of rejection. The man on the bench, Joe is his name. Joe asked me what was wrong and if he could pray for me? Many would label Joe as a very different fellow, perhaps a square peg? He easily bothers people some avoid him. He may not be easy to understand with his Hungarian accent, unless you really sit down and listen to what he is saying. Joe has been rejected many times. He has been looked down upon, shunned by many. Yet it was Joe who noticed my sadness and cared enough to ask what was wrong? In God's ironic way of working, God used Joe to minister to me. God used someone who knows how it feels to be unwanted, to minister to me when I felt unwanted. God ministered through the unloved, when I felt unloved. God worked through the rejected to minister to me, when I felt rejected. God revealed Himself through the Hebrew Christian known as Hungarian Joe.

God will also work through you and He will work through me, to minister to others in His most perfect way. God changes our hearts through these life experiences. That is how we become more like Jesus. When we know how it feels, we are less likely to treat others in that manner which would cause such sadness.

2Corinthians 1:3 & 4 "Praise be to the God and Father of our Lord Jesus Christ, the Father of compassion and the God of all comfort, who comforts us in all our troubles, so that we can comfort those in any trouble with the comfort we ourselves have received from God."

One day when I was praying to God about a similar situation, I waited for an answer. I wrote down this message I believe God replied to me:

"There is no condemnation in Christ Jesus. Wherever you decide to go, go in Christ's Love. To be in His Perfect Will is to be in His Perfect Love. Perfect love cast out all fear. There

can be no doubt, no wavering when you build my church. There is no perfect church because my children take their eyes off me. If your eyes remained on me then there would be Unity that is unbreakable. When my children seek some counsel from others first, instead of seeking the counsel from the Almighty Counselor, doors of deception are opened and my children are easily deceived. Dust of depravity enters into my church, (corruption, perversion, wickedness, gossip, judgement). When this happens, my church can flounder. Remember who your enemy is. He will surely try to tear down my church, especially in the stage of new birth. You cannot grow strong as a church body unless you are fed and get your nutrition from God the Father, through the Son Christ Jesus. He is the cornerstone, the foundation and also the head of each church. He is the source which makes all things flourish." In the end there is always good in every situation. As long as we seek God and His direction, He will reveal to us that good and perfect will. The victory belongs to Jesus. God will show us how to best use what we have learned from life's experiences, for His glory. There is a saying, "Do unto others, as you would have others do unto you." It is an attitude worth trying to live. Sometimes, God has to rub hard on those square edges, so we can fit into those round holes.

Square Peg in a Round Hole
CHAPTER 31

1. Have you ever felt like a square peg in a round hole? What did you do to try and fit?

2. Read 2 Timothy 1:7. Has fear had a grip on you? What task has fear prevented you from accomplishing?

3. What destroys fear?

4. Read Joshua 1:9. What does God command us to do in the sight of fear? What encouragement do we have from God?

5. Sometimes we suffer trials, but we learn from our trials. From reading 2 Corinthians 1:3-4, What should we do with what we learn from these experiences?

6. Read the poem on page 207. When I read John 8:1-11, I can imagine Jesus bending down and drawing that circle and writing in the dirt, "You are forgiven." What correlation do you recognize between the two stories?

32

The Champions
Take Me Out to the Ball Game

It is the championship game, bottom of the seventh inning. The winning run is on third base; two out and you are up to bat. The fans are cheering, your teammates are yelling, "You can do it. Take the pitch you want." "Come on, hit him home." The pressure is intense, emotions riding high. Your heart is pounding. The other team is yelling and encouraging their pitcher. The umpire roars, "play ball." In comes the pitch. It's a good one. You swing, contact is made and the ball is sailing through the air. Oh No, it is hanging up. The fielder is running. Is she going to catch it? The crowd grows deathly quiet in anticipation. Both teams know that this is the winning play of the game. Which team will cheer? Will it be the one who catches the ball or the one who sees the ball drop? Time stands still. Three cheers, Hip Hip Hurray! Hip Hip Hurray!

This year it was our turn to win the championship. For a few minutes the excitement and emotions ran high. We, the team accomplished our goal. We were successful. Batting averages were high. Errors kept at a minimum. Winning average for the season was 99%. Our team did well according to baseball statistics.

The team: nine players, two spares and a couple of coaches. "What made this team successful?" I asked myself. The team consisted of many different levels of ball players. Some players have played baseball for twenty or thirty years and are very skilled. For others it was their first or second year. They were skilled with enthusiasm, stemmed from their fresh young blood.

This team had heart, a will to win, character to never give up and the comradery to push each other to do our very best. I guess what stand out the most, is that we knew how to make playing baseball fun. We were a team in every sense of the word. We worked together, encouraged each other. We played despite our injuries and gave it all we had to give, using our skills to the best of our ability. I guess that is the difference between victory and defeat. For this year we are "The Champions" and enjoying the victory very much. We are a team proud of what was achieved. Next year is another season. Maybe we will have a different team roster? For now we enjoy our victory. Tomorrow is another day. I think it is human nature to want to be on a winning team or even just be on a team. It gives one a sense of belonging. When you are on a team, you are not a lone ranger. There is something special about being on a team. We feel it when we watch soldiers put up the victory flag. It is a feeling which gathers millions of people together in a stadium and in front of our television sets, to cheer on a team. When our team loses, we feel the agony of defeat. When our team wins, we feel tears of victory. It is an unexplainable feeling when we watch the World Series Champions, as they run and jump on top of each other. We feel like we are there with them, as they pat each other on the back and hug. We celebrate with them the win of the game, as they carry the trophy up high. For most of us it sparks excitement and motivation.

Team work is not a new concept. It has been around for

thousands of years. They had chariot races and games in arenas dating back to time before Christ. It has always been human nature to be competitive. The Apostle Paul looked at life as a race. Facing persecution, imprisonment and hardships, he had the desire to continue.

Paul writes, *Acts 20:24 "However, I consider my life worth nothing to me, if only I may finish the race and complete the task the Lord Jesus has given me - the task of testifying to the gospel of God's grace."*

The Holy Spirit gave Paul direction, a task and a goal. Paul had the determination to complete that goal and nothing else mattered. Paul's perspective and goal were toward the eternal. He says in

1 Corinthians. 9:24 "Do you not know that in a race all the runners run, but only one gets the prize? Run in such a way as to get the prize."

I think of Paul's perspective on life, being like a race. Paul was talking about spiritual lessons. We can certainly apply his advice to anything in life, even the way we play a baseball game. Often I compare the spiritual with the everyday events, for example our baseball team. I think of the success of our baseball team. It makes me wonder how we as a team of Christians can achieve that same victory? I think of our ball team, with nine players, two spares and a couple of coaches. The nine players all played a different position. Infielders, outfielders, catcher, pitcher and two spare players just in case someone was injured or couldn't play. We had to have all players present at the game or we would lose by default. Those are the rules of the league, written in the baseball handbook.

Now let's look at life in the spiritual sense in accordance with the league rules of life. God has given us a major league handbook written out for us. It is the Holy Bible.

Paul speaks about a team of players. He calls this team, "The Body of Christ." *Romans 12:4-8.*

"Just as each of us has one body with many members, and these members do not all have the same function, so in Christ we who are many form one body, and each member belongs to all the others. We have different gifts, according to the grace given us. If a man's gift is prophesying, let him use it in proportion to his faith. If it is serving, let him serve; if it is teaching, let him teach; if it is encouraging, let him encourage; if it is contributing to the needs of others, let him give generously; if it is leadership, let him govern diligently; if it is showing mercy, let him do it cheerfully."

When I read that scripture, the game sounds very easy. When a team is put together with players who have these gifts, all we have to do is let them play their position according to how God has gifted them. So, we have a starting line up:

Coach - Leader
Pitcher - Server,
1st base - Prophesier,
2nd base - Faith,
3rd base - Teacher,
Short Stop - Encourager,
Back Catcher - Governor,
Outfielders - Diligent, Mercy, and Cheerful.
Don't forget the spares - Willing and Able.

On a successful team we all drink from the same water bottle. *1 Corinthians 12:13. "For we were all baptized by one Spirit into one body whether Jew or Greeks, slave or free and we were all given the one Spirit to drink."*

Whether we are on a baseball team, a hockey team or the team called "The Body of Christ." Victory only comes when we work together and be a team.

The Champions
CHAPTER 32

1. For more on the body of Christ read 1 Corinthians. 12:12-28.

2. Jesus began a team, when he started recruiting His twelve disciples, (Luke 6:12-15) What were the names of the first 12 disciples?

3. Read Matthew 10:1-19. Jesus calls the disciples and gives them His game plan. What was the first thing Jesus gave the disciples to equip them to be on His team?

4. What did that authority give them power to do?

5. Every coach gives a game plan. What did Jesus instruct the disciples to do?

6. In Matthew 10:16-19. Jesus says He is sending them out like sheep among wolves. What does Jesus warn them about?

7. What does that mean to be as shrewd as snakes and as innocent as doves?

8. What assurance or comfort does Jesus give to his disciples in Matthew 10 :19 and 20?

9. Even today Jesus equips His disciples. Read 2 Timothy 3:16-17. What has Jesus given to us that will help us play our position in the body of Christ and equip us for every good work?

33

The Fight
"A friend loves at all times"

A baby was born. The labour pain was intense. That little baby fought all the way into this world. Some day as that baby grows into a senior, the day will come when it will take that last breath. That human body will probably fight to the end. It is human instinct. The response to fight is born into us.

I was talking to a friend one day. She was having a hard time with one of her friendships. She was feeling stressed and angry with a close friend and they had been arguing. They got caught up in the fight and began to put each other down, insult and judge each other. She said to me, "best friends don't treat each other that way." She began to question their friendship.

I thought about her statement. It reminded me of a story I remembered from years ago. I still smell the fresh long grass and cool fresh breezes from the lake. I remember the laughter that seems to ring so loudly in my ears even now, as I reminisce. There was a family that lived across the street. They had a few boys and six girls in the family. My two older brothers hung around with Jim and Leonard and a couple of other boys in the neighbourhood. In age, the girls were all about a year and a half apart. I played often with one or the other. Lou Ann and I played together more often than the others. She was a year older than I. Even then, I never knew what close friends we were to each other. I only realized this after we had the biggest fight ever.

This particular night we were all together playing baseball in the neighbor's yard. Whack, as the sound of the baseball hit the bat. We would run around the boat cushions we used for bases. Lou Ann was up to bat. The baseball game was so much fun. Our team was winning. We were cheering each other on. However, Lou Ann was not on my team this time. We were opposing each other. I was pitching and I struck her out. This meant that it was now my turn up to bat. She did not want to give up her turn at bat. I barely recall what happened, but the next thing I knew we started fighting over the bat. Next, I was on the ground and she was on top of me pulling my hair, scratching and punching me. Next thing I knew, her big brother Jim pulled her off of me. However, the fight did not stop. We started fighting again and this time I was pulling hair, and punching her back. Her sisters were cheering, "Get her Becky!" They were cheering for me. Heart broken and hurt, Lou Ann went home crying. Everyone else was still standing around and the game came to an end. Her sister congratulated me on winning the fight. My brother was quick to notice my head had a big gouge in it and I was bleeding. I remember I felt like crying too, as my heart ached. I wouldn't cry with everyone standing around. So, I quickly went into my house and broke out in sobs. My brother was quick to tell me what a big baby I was. My Mum bandaged up my forehead and hugged me and that made me feel better.

The next morning it was time to go to school and go to the bus stop. Time to face my foe or face my friend. I didn't want to go. I didn't know what I would say! What would she say? Would she beat me up again? I feared the unknown. Away I went, as my mother sent me out the door. Lou Ann was waiting at the bus stop. Sheepishly, I walked up to her. For a few moments, we looked at each other with our blank troublesome faces.

Dumbfounded, we both broke out in laughter at our plight then we hugged each other and reconciled. After that day, Lou Ann and I never fought again. I was only eight years old and she was nine at the time. I think that day we became best of friends. Not because we fought, although the fight reinforced the true hearts of love we shared between us. Perhaps it was more about our childlike perspectives on life. We lived for that day and we instinctively knew how to reconcile. Children seem to forgive and forget quickly. Always ready to move forward and get back to having fun. A few months later, Lou Ann and her family moved away. I will never forget that fight. Within those brief moments of fighting, it seemed we lost sight of each other. For a moment our pride, anger and self-protecting nature took over with such intent to injure. Mostly it brings a smile and a warm touch to my heart, to remember how we made up, how we forgave, and how we could really see each other and get beyond that fight. We never held that fight against each other. Our lives took different paths. I still see Lou Ann once every few years. We laugh about it. As bad as it was, it has become a great memory.

I think of life and those memories, when time does seem to stand still. Our old neighbourhood is gone. The houses have changed in appearance. In a strange way, it was like another life. It was a great life. So, I look at time as it passes by, remembering the people who drift in and out of our lives. In general I think of relationships of every kind. There are so many things that can rob people of rich full and wonderful relationships. I was thinking about the people in my life at this present time. I love them so much. But it is easy to take them for granted.

We all say things to each other, seldom do we think of the possibility of not seeing them tomorrow. It never crosses our minds that the people we love might not be here the next time we go to call.

I've seen the lives of people change in what seems like a snap of the fingers. When that happens, it becomes too late for regrets - too late to take back words they wish they had never spoken. It is then too late to say something you wish you had said. It is like all the misunderstandings and disagreements become meaningless. They no longer matter. You wonder why you wasted the opportunities of life to enjoy the game because you fought over whose turn it was to bat. All you would like back is that brother or sister, mum, dad or friend. You would gladly give them their turn at the bat. Just for the chance to have them back, you would probably have the bat gold plated for them.

Life does have a curve ball. We can't always hit home runs. Sometimes we even strike out. We play the game of life like a baseball game. Hopefully nobody charges the mound. Even if they do, we can be like that childlike spirit and forgive and forget and even laugh about it. It reminds me of that song. "That's the story of that's the glory of love." In the realm of eternity, the little fights and disagreements are just trivial in comparison. People and relationships are more important. I guess it is a lesson in appreciation. It is one lesson I hope we never have to learn the hard way.

To my friend, I encourage you to walk to that bus stop and conquer fear and pride. Go give your friend a hug. Maybe that hug will ignite a happy memory both of you will laugh about many years from now - a memory that can change your lives, attitudes and your friendship.

The Fight
CHAPTER 33

1. The book of Proverbs is full of wise sayings. Read the following Proverbs and write them down or discuss them with a group?

Proverbs 17:14 - "Starting a quarrel is like breaching a dam; so drop the matter before a dispute breaks out."

Proverbs 16:32 - "Better a patient man than a warrior, a man who controls his temper than one who takes a city."

Proverbs 17:22 - "A cheerful heart is good medicine, but a crushed spirit dries up the bones."

Proverbs 17:28 - "Even a fool is thought wise if he keeps silent, and discerning if he holds his tongue."

Proverbs 17:17 - "A friend loves at all times, and a brother is born for adversity."

Proverbs 18:12 - "Before his downfall a man's heart is proud, but humility comes before honour."

Proverbs 16:22 - "Understanding is a fountain of life to those who have it, but folly brings punishment to fools."

2. Do you have any areas in your life which you could apply these proverbs too? Discuss how you can make an application?

34

The Mask

❧

**. . . Satan himself masquerades as an angel of light.
2 Corinthians 11:14**

I s the world one big masquerade party? Daily we see
people masquerade behind a mask of pretending imagery
trying to be accepted by the status quo. Why do we think we
have to hide our real identities and personalities behind a
mask? Is there so much fear of rejection in the world, or just
too much rejection? Why do we persist in the game? What
does it take to be who God created us to be? Will the real
John Doe please stand up?

Without saying much babble, the direction I would point
you to is to the Almighty Counselor, Jesus Christ. It is
crucial that we as children of God know our identity in Him.
By knowing, believing and having faith in Him, we can
learn to accept the fact that God totally accepts us and we
are exactly who God created us to be. He formed us in our
mother's wombs.

Let us look behind the masks; remembering that the first
mask we need to remove is the one we are wearing. Have you
ever experienced relationships where it has taken more than
a couple years before you get to know the person behind the

mask? Perhaps years have passed and you realized one day that you never even knew the person you called your neighbour, brother, spouse or friend. The masks wear out over time and fall off. Have you ever experienced a broken relationship? The mask is off and your relationship has ended.

You are left holding a mask full of questions and tears. We wonder what on earth happened, surprised by the mask of deception we never knew existed. When we try to build our relationships, it is important to build the foundation with real materials like honesty, love, reality and truth. Any imitation materials will not persevere the stormy weather ahead.

If we look at an imitation flower compared with a flower filled with life, what might we notice? From a distance both look the same. Some imitation flowers look so real, you cannot tell until you touch or smell them. Nothing can replace the natural beauty of a flower, fragrant fresh with silky softness and vivid colours. Without the fragrance something is missing. They are beautiful on the outside yet fragrant less, never growing or spreading life. No seeds can fall from an imitation. Even sun and rain will not enhance its beauty. In fact sun and rain will only enhance the fraudulent reality of the emptiness held within a stem without roots. Without growth, without life, it is dead. In the same way God's light will eventually reveal the things in our lives, which are imitation. Truth will always uncover the lie.

We frequently hear on the news about horrendous crimes committed. People are left in disbelief of the offender. We cannot believe our neighbour could have done such a crime. After all, he was such a nice guy. We are left shocked. I always wonder, did anyone ever really take the time to get to know the person behind the mask? Maybe he had been crying out for such a long time. No one noticed, or cared enough to help or listen to the cry behind the mask. Does that make us accomplices to the crimes?

The originality of these masks began a long time ago in the Garden of Eden. God had created everything perfect and it was all very good. The first mask maker was Satan, who was also in the garden. Satan the devil gave Eve the first mask as a lie. He told Eve what God had given her was not enough. She needed more.

Eve swallowed the lie along with the fruit from the forbidden tree. Today we are still swallowing Satan's lies. You have to be funny. Your nose is too big. You have to drink, take drugs, smoke to be part of the crowd. They will not like you if . . . And on and on the lies go. Satan wears the craftiest mask of all. The bible says that Satan masquerades as an angel of light. He would like nothing better than for us to wear his masks and be like him, deceiving and being deceived.

We have not lost. There is victory in Christ Jesus. We can learn from the mistake Eve made and we can learn from the mistakes we make. It is time to take off the mask and be who God created us to be. Allow God to change us into His image. In the changing process learn to accept and praise God for who we are in Christ Jesus. In Christ, we are so much more than the surface appearance. Behind every face is a beautiful spirit and soul that God loves so very much. He is waiting to shine out and shine in and melt off the masks of deception. He wants to end the masquerade party. Jesus never hid behind any mask. He made no false pretences. Christ lived truth all the way to the cross, the grave and back to heaven. Praise God. Be real! Be free! Be all that God intended us to be!

The Mask
CHAPTER 34

1. What are the names of Satan? (Deuteronomy 13:13, Matthew 10:25, 1 John 3:8, 12:30, Luke 8:30,)

2. What are some characteristics of Satan? (Genesis 1, 3:1, Job 1:6-12, 2:1-6, Revelation 12:10)

3. Who are you in Christ Jesus?

4. One of the main ways Satan tries to attack us, is in our thoughts. Study these scriptures and write down how we can battle and defeat Satan and his tactics. (2 Corinthians 10:5, Romans 12:1-2, James 5:16, Psalm 150:6)

5. Read Revelation 12:11 and write down the key way in which we can overcome Satan?

Remove the negative thoughts and replace them with the word of God and His truth. Prayer is important because your relationship with the Lord will grow in intimacy and His power will strengthen, protect and free you. Praise is also a big weapon against Satan.

35

An Angel of Hope
Wings of Courage

Sometimes in life we must fly on the wings of courage. These are wings of divine strength, to persevere the trials along the road to perfection. It might be a physical battle against a deadly disease or a battle of a broken heart. Perhaps your trial is a family divided by divorce. Is it coping with the death of a loved one? Have you lost your job, to which you dedicated twenty-five years of your life? Whatever the trial, they put us in a place where we must totally rely on God for strength, trusting that He will work everything out for good. Just when our circumstance seems worse than anyone else's, they tap out all of our hope and strength. God sends an angel of hope.

One day while I was caught in the depths of my despair, God sent me an angel named Jenny. I don't think Jenny is a real angel in the true sense of the word. Nevertheless, all who have met Jenny in all her qualities describe her as such an angel. Jenny is a precious little girl of five years old. She is a wonderful little girl full of vibrant life and strength. Jenny, like all children, speaks such truthful messages.

We watch our children play, run and jump. Their laughter

brings a joy and happiness to our spirits that is really indescribable. If you have children of your own, you know what I'm talking about. I remember watching my children grow from babies through to adolescents, each stage unique.

Life is a journey through different stages.
   Transforming and adapting.
      God directs us through the valleys.
         Over the mountains.

Quiet and innocent.
   The baby survives miraculously.
      With vitality, propelling motion,
         A baby's life begins.

Setting the first stage.
   Gasping and crying a baby is born.
      Into a new world.
         Learning to inhale that first breath.

Setting the second stage.
   Sitting, walking, running and jumping.
      The baby becomes a toddler.
         A child constantly coping with each transition.

Setting the third stage.
   Racing hormones, new emotions.
      Creating a collage of ideas.
         Becoming more independent.
            Physically, spiritually, emotionally.

Setting the fourth stage.
   Stepping out on their own.
      Creating a new circle, adult to adult.
         Another baby is born.

Setting the fifth stage.
  Connecting circles.
    Parenting love with experience.
      Passing wisdom to those lower in the circle.

Setting the final stage.
  Generations slowly pass away.
    Circles keep on multiplying.
      Like a chain, intertwined.
        Never ending circles.

Each first step, new word, creates an excitement. We are proud of our children. So, we move through life growing in many ways with our children. We thank God for the blessings they are in our lives. Eventually the days turn into years as the sands of time sift through the hourglass and again time stands still.

What about the broken cycles of life? There are a select group or few who are an exception to the rule. These are children who never reach adulthood. Some would label them the special ones. They are courageous, strong in spirit, yet physically sick with diseases like cancer, AIDS, cystic fibrosis etc. Other rare diseases like neurofibromatosis II attack children like Jenny. Diseases that are not very familiar. Tumours on the eighth cranial nerve, which can lead to hearing loss, headaches, problems with facial movements, problems with balance, and difficulty walking and more, characterize this disease.

Jenny is one of these special children. Do you know someone like Jenny? Sometimes we wonder why God allows these little children to suffer. Why doesn't God heal them and answer our prayers? These questions crossed my mind as my heart broke for little Jenny while I prayed. Jenny has severe scoliosis with a severe curvature of her spine. She needs a special therapeutic brace to keep her back supported. Along the base of her spine she has more than thirty tumours that draw strength and nutrients from her bones and body. These tumours cause her constant pain all day every day. Jenny also has a hole in her heart. Specialists all around the world have never seen anything like Jenny's case study of this disease. Jenny also has a second strain of this rare disease, which is at work in her little body. Amazingly, this second strain could create a cure for leukemia, but because of the condition of Jenny's heart and the tumours, the needed operations could cause Jenny to bleed to death. Her case is very different and very much confidential with the government and medical research.

There is hope through Jenny that could save millions of lives in the future. Until more research is done, Jenny has no choice but to persevere through her pain. Except for the tears that run down her face while she watches cartoons, Jenny is always smiling and a very happy and courageous little girl.

Jenny smiles and laughs, coping very well with the pain from this disease. She is such a wonderful example to everyone around her, demonstrating perseverance and great disposition.

Maybe God allows these physically weak children to display His inner strength? Jenny and children like her are an inspiration to me. I see how happy they are in spite of the illnesses and the battle they have for life. God speaks through Jenny to those of us who suffer with depression and oppression. The message I received is that things could always be worse.

Can we empathize with the parents of Jenny? They watch Jenny constantly, never knowing what the future holds for their little girl. They do everything humanly possible to make sure Jenny has the best care. Jenny's mother is now involved in an organization to bring more awareness to such diseases. She is lobbying for more rights for donors like Jenny and for more governmental intervention, to bring about testing of these tumours, which could help find a cure. Until that happens, one of those tumours sits frozen in a research laboratory. The biggest challenges and decisions are still ahead. Do they consent to many more tests and operations, which could be fatal for Jenny? Do they sacrifice the life of their little girl to find a cure that could save the lives of many others who suffer with this deadly disease? What decision would you make if this were your child?

We pray for divine guidance as we make these decisions. We pray for Jenny, for the doctors, government leaders and medical research. We pray for God's perfect will to be done, hoping, trusting and believing that the outcome will be miraculous. Remember, Jesus' desperate prayer, as He also had to look ahead to the pain, torment and persecution He knew He would have to endure.

Again we see the love of a heavenly Father, making an extremely difficult decision. His son Jesus had to die so that many could live. They remind us of the willingness and perseverance Jesus experienced.

Most of us have all heard of similar cases to Jenny. To many of us, these tragic life cases are interesting conversation or the news of the day. We must never forget that to every Jenny there is a precious little face, a real person with real needs. They need our prayers, not our talk. A prayer of faith can help Jenny and children like her, through the days ahead.

At this time Jenny has endured her first set of operations. There are many more to follow. She has so much to overcome. According to the doctors' diagnoses, she may not walk again. Her heart needs an operation and the tumours could grow and spread anywhere in her little body. Jenny is engaged in a battle for her life. You can help her with your prayers. Miracles happen and through our prayers nothing is impossible, when we put our trust in Jesus.

The name Jenny has been changed to legally protect her identity and her family. God knows Jenny's real identity. We lift this little angel of hope up to God in prayer and ask for a miracle cure.

Amen.

Study questions are with chapter 36.

36

Message of Faith

God Spoke through a Bush
God can speak through a man.

One weekend, while I was away at a retreat for women, I met a ranch hand. I was sitting in the basement where they had the services, playing my guitar and worshipping Jesus. A ranch hand named Joe walked up to me. He started giving me this message from the Lord. He began by talking to me about faith. Joe, a messenger of God perhaps. He was definitely too humble to call himself a prophet, yet Joe was obedient enough to speak out to me what he believed God wanted to tell me. This is the message he spoke to me. Maybe His message will challenge your faith, the same way it challenged mine?

Joe spoke: "If you were to throw a tissue on the floor, how much faith would it take? If you were to pick the tissue up off the floor, how much faith would it take? God says, with that very same faith, you can go to a mountain and say, go throw yourself into the sea and it will. The moral of the story is that if you have this much faith or that much faith they can both do the very same thing. This much faith is not *any more powerful than this much faith because the faith is eternal, which makes you eternal.*

If you have Jesus as your Saviour, the sovereign Lord of Hosts sovereignly anoints you. He dwells inside of you. Jesus Christ is inside you. He is eternal. He has made you now eternal. Meaning He wants you to think eternal, walk eternal. When you reach out and grab somebody, it is eternal. You are eternal living in a temporal realm. Because you are eternal, that makes you sovereign.

Meaning that if a demon were to run past you right now, he would have to fall down and bow at your feet before he could carry on. Meaning, he cannot go to God and say: "Well I do not feel like it right now, God. The scripture reference for that is Luke 5:1-20. Jesus gets off the boat after crossing the sea. There is a man demon possessed up in tombs about a half-mile off. When Jesus hits the land, the man sees Him, runs down the hill, falls before His feet. The demons speak out of the man and say, "Jesus Son of the Most High God. We know who you are. Please don't destroy us, but let us go over to those pigs over there."

They had to submit. The thing to understand now, in eternal meaning, your days never end. However, Satan's days are marked. He is temporal. You are eternal. So what he does is try to get you to look at the size of the thing you are praying for. Oh he says. "You do not have enough faith." They call it intimidation. He intimidates you. You pray and pray and pray and pray. However, these things do not happen. Why? God says, "Well you know. You speak to it." But God, I do not have enough faith. Who told you, you don't have enough faith? The accuser of the brethren says you do not have enough faith. So who told you, you do not have enough faith? No, no, no! You have enough faith, wisdom, hope, all the gifts of God, and all the qualities of God, within His character to sustain you eternally. So when you go to God and you say: "Hey God, I need more faith, I need more wisdom."

God is saying you need to ask me the real question. Because all the things you are asking me for, you already have in its fullness. The fullness of the day He dwells in bodily form. Father, Son and Holy Spirit live right in you. All right, you need to be asking God for understanding. Man can only understand the things of God, by the Spirit of God. He cannot possess or claim ownership of the things of God. He can only understand and through understanding the issues of faith, then man will speak with tongues of fire." This is a thought-provoking message.

Understanding the issues of faith, we are reminded that a seed planted in a crack on a rock can grow into a tree that can split that rock in two. God knows all things. Abide in God. It may be a miracle of the ages. "The works that I do shall ye do also and greater works than these shall ye do because I go to My Father." The lame walked, the blind received sight and the lepers were healed.

By the power of the Holy Spirit we too, can experience God's healing in our lives. "Ask what you will, and it shall be done for you" and for those for whom we pray. Do you believe?

Angel of Hope -
Message of Faith
CHAPTER 35 AND 36

1. We read of many miracles throughout the Bible. Mark 9:1-29. This boy had an evil spirit. How was this boy healed and what was the method Jesus specifically said would free or heal this child?

2. Why do you think the disciples wanted more faith? How much faith does Jesus suggest they need to accomplish great feats?
(Luke 17:5-7 also Matthew 13:31-32, Mark 4:31)

3. Many people have questioned my encounter I had with Joe, a man of wisdom and insight. Does God still use men as prophets the way He did in the Old Testament? It is always important to check the spirit?
(John 7:16-19)

4. Study (1 Corinthians 12:7-11). What are the gifts of the Spirit mentioned?

5. A miracle is an action that cannot be explained by natural means. In Acts 3 Peter heals a crippled beggar. What method did Peter use by which this man was healed? By whose authority did they heal?

6. Acts 3:16 - What two things does Peter say healed this man?

In the name of Jesus of Nazareth, please pray for Jenny everyday for one month or as long as you feel the Holy Spirit prompting you to pray. Believe for a miracle healing for this little angel of hope.

37

Bright Lights in a Big City

Letting your little light shine

Here we go! For those of you who want to come along. "Where are we going?" You asked! La . . . La . . . La . . . Nevada. Okay, I'll say it quietly, so I am not quickly condemned or persecuted. We are going to Las Vegas. Shhhhhh! Come aboard flight 629 and I'll tell you about my trip. I'll just skip over the justification of me going to, what some would call a modern day Sodom and Gomorrah or "Sin City." Was it a free trip? Or did it cost me my soul? Did you ask me if I fell into temptation? My answer is yes. My flesh did give in to putting a few nickels into the slot machine, if that equates sin? Did I feel condemnation or was it conviction with each pull of the one-armed bandits? There is a difference. Condemnation is from Satan. Conviction is from the Lord. If you know what a one-armed bandit is, then you have probably been to Las Vegas or a place just like it.

A spectacular blend of neon lights lit up the sky with a

beautiful array of every different light bulb invented by man. It is an architectural magnificence of replica cities like Paris, Belachio, Venice and New York. Attractive casinos like Caesar's Palace decorate their halls with giant statues of mythical Gods. The closest thing I saw to a biblical idea was a nude statue. It was a twenty five-foot tall interpretation of King David holding a sling, ready to kill the giant.

When I wasn't getting caught in the trap of the game, I was people-watching, thinking and reminiscing about my teen years when I first visited this town. I seemed destined to go there. This was about my tenth time visiting Vegas.

Planeload after planeload of people arrive to win mega bucks only to depart tired with empty pockets or a suitcase full of souvenirs. Sure, occasionally some lucky soul hits a jackpot. That is if you believe in luck. Luck is the key word thrown around. What is Vegas? Entertainment, yes! As I watched the people, the portrayal of some, was that of the greed-motivated robots, numbed and perverted by the game. Others were enjoying themselves, having fun in the mirage of an adult Disney World. Some would say Las Vegas is a nice vacation or mere entertainment and recreation. Is it? I could not help but notice hearing many ambulance sirens. It was like a bad TV show that keeps showing reruns. I kept wondering what it was; heart attack victims or suicide cases?

Going to Vegas reminds me a little bit of Pinocchio the puppet. Remember when he innocently tags along with his new friend, they go to the land of plenty? We know what happened to Pinocchio and his friend. They turned into donkeys. Pinocchio escaped just in time.

While in Vegas, it was one of those moments when time stands still, for a few days. We were in this new world, caught up in the mirage. There was no evidence of spiritual stimulation and morality appeared low. Children stood on the street and gave out booklets of nude women to the passers by. I saw no sign of a church. The closest thing to a church was the chapel where a rent-a-ref performs a quick marriage in the name of the State of Nevada. (Rent-a-ref is the nickname for justice of the peace)

Over the last few days, what was really brought to my mind was the extreme paradox between darkness and light. In both cases we see people who are on a personal quest for whatever fills their desires or needs. For some it is power or money. What form of transportation we take; to reach our destination is questionable? In our quest for spiritual enlightenment sometimes we get lost on a spiritual crusade all of our own. Sometimes it seems like Christians are the ones on a different planet, caught in religiosity. By the secular world I've been accused of being on some spiritual quest.

My Christian family has told me that I'm not there yet. Guess what? I am and I am not! I have been on both planets and can see both can be damaging. There is bondage in both. Can darkness dwell with light? Jesus accomplished this balance all the time. Going to Las Vegas may not be a spiritually enlightened place to visit. By going there it revealed the reality of this world in which we live. What God is trying to show us, is the broader picture of life. With our human perception, we could probably look down and see a big sinful city filled with so many lights that our little Christian light is very dim. Do you ever feel like a Waldo light, hidden away by all that surrounds you? Reality is, through Christ Jesus we are lights not to be overlooked, yet not so spiritually bright that we out-shine all the man-made extravaganzas of lights.

We must all find that place God has for us in this world. It does not matter whether we are surrounded by the world's population or sitting under a tree all alone reading a book. There is a place for each of us. God is talking to us always. We just have to try to listen in the crowd, listen in the silence and learn to distinguish the voice of God. We must be careful not to get caught on a magic carpet ride of false spiritual self-gratification. This could be a trap of pride, telling us we are more spirit-filled than others. Spiritual snob syndrome could set in. Symptoms are; swollen head and inflated ego. We are children of God. Like a father talks to his children, God talks to us. It is simple. We don't need to be a prophet, a teacher, or someone who heals or raises the dead, unless God directs us to do so. These things would be nice. In reality, these things don't make us any more special or spiritual. The only one who can make us anything is God Himself. All the prophetic classes in the world can't raise a prophet. Only God can do that. Was my trip to Las Vegas futile, sinful? I think not. Among the clanging machines, sirens and smoky air, God was speaking to me. I was trying to listen. I'll chalk Las Vegas up to another desert experience. Las Vegas Nevada is a city in the desert. Was it all just a mirage of "Bright Lights in a Big City?" Or was it a wake-up call, to the reality of a people caught in a matrix of darkness hidden by Bright lights in a big city?

Big Lights In the Big City
CHAPTER 37

1. Read Philippians 2:12-18. God is a God in whom we find great love, compassion, and comfort. But, He is also the God whom we must obey with deep reverence and fear.

2. What is the believer's part? How does a believer work out his/her salvation?

3. What part does God have in our salvation?

4. (Philippians. 2:14-18) Where are we to shine our lights? How are we to shine our light? (Matthew 5:14-16)

5. Jesus is the light of the world, the truth. Jesus talks about the light on a lamp stand.
   (Luke 8:16 -18). What does the light represent as Christians?

6. Read about the lamp of the body. (Luke 11:34 - 36). What is Jesus saying about light and darkness? How can a person who is surrounded by darkness keep a pure light shining?
   "His Love . . . Let it shine through me"

7. In what ways might the light dispense in so many colours throughout the world?

38

Lost in a Field of Dreams

❦

**But those who hope in the Lord will renew their
strength. They will soar on wings like eagles;
they will run and not grow weary,
they will walk and not be faint.
Isaiah 40:31**

There was a tantalizing fragrance lingering in the air
from the Fall harvest. The smell of Fall tingled one's
senses with a light breeze flowing through the air. It was a
brilliantly warm day with the sun shining and not a cloud in
the sky. Trees hung lazily inward lining the edge of a quiet
dirt road. It almost seemed like the trees were leading us
toward my husband's Mom and Dad's farm. Majestic leaves
shimmered in the light breeze. An awesome painting of
greens mixed with a slight touch of yellow, orange and red.
The branches swayed back and forth like a mother rocking
her baby. There was quietness in the day, which left one with
a strange feeling of wonderment.

The season was beginning to change. Each cool night
left its mark in the appearance of each new day, with each
subtle metamorphosis. It was like a signature written in the
colors - a period at the end of a sentence, so a new sentence,

or a new day could begin.

It was Sept 12, 1990, one of the last warm weekends to mark the end of another hot summer past. But for our family the end of this summer would be etched in our minds for many seasons to follow. In the quiet of each day, we all have different perspectives on life, according to what is happening in our lives at that time. Now I wonder what perspective Steve had that day? These kinds of questions will always be unanswered, lost in a timeless day when time stood still.

The farm, it always had an atmosphere all of it's own. Mom and Dad had to retire from farming because Dad had a heart attack earlier in the year. My brothers' in-law Mike and Steve did a little plowing to help out. No cows to milk, just a couple hundred acres to plow, and get ready for Fall. On any other day the farm would be a place one could call home, peaceful, quiet, accept for the odd tractor. On that fateful September 12, 1990, the farm was more than just a couple hundred of acres for Steve to plow. It was his ocean of emptiness. Alone, feeling rejected, humiliated, Steve was lost in overwhelming despair. Steve was swallowed by a dark cloud of depression that impaired him from seeing anything, but a means to an end. For Steve, his plan may have seemed like a way to end all his heartfelt pain, which was apparently too much for him to cope with anymore.

Steve was in the middle of a separation from his wife, his children and his home. His life as he lived it, was falling apart and it seemed there was no way he could put things back together. These factors and others may have left him with a sense of gloom and doom?

At the time I was a young Christian still developing my thoughts and courage. Many times as I listened to Steve pour out his heart, I wanted to say something that would give him hope, encouragement. I said many things. I can still remember a conversation we had about suicide that week. In a strange sort of way, I could relate to how Steve was feeling. There have been times when I have struggled with depression, rejection and similar feelings. I remember saying "Yea, I know how you feel Steve. Sometimes, I have had suicidal thoughts. I wouldn't follow them through though." Steve spoke with determination by saying. "Well, I would. I would do it." Then our conversation faded to something else. At times I have felt like kicking myself, thinking maybe there was something more helpful I could have said and done. I could have told him that it is Jesus who gets me through my struggles. Possibly I could have related to Steve that when I feel so depressed, I pray. When I do, Jesus in some way shows me the way up out of the pit of despair.

I didn't say a word of truth about Jesus to Steve. Probably I feared what his reaction might be? Simply, it was not about me, but my thoughts should have been about him. My faith at that time was not strong enough to share Jesus Christ with him. Maybe I should have said something. Maybe I could have said something more. I didn't. Little did I know at the time that it would soon be too late. I'm sure many of us have struggled since, wondering if we could have made a difference. The fact is, it does not matter now, because we cannot change the past. It is not healthy to continue to blame ourselves. These are burdens, which we must give to Jesus. That is how we can continue the healing process and grieve our loss.

On that last day of summer, it was the typical norm where everyone seemed to have something to do that day. My family was having a barbeque. Mom and Dad had some visiting to do and Mike had his own work to do at his home. Steve seemed to be doing his own thing and just hanging around the farm. He said he might go visit a friend. So, we all went our separate ways and Steve stayed back at the farm by himself. He locked his car up, made one last phone call and then only God knows what went through his mind on that quiet day. The farm is a big place when you are feeling very small and insignificant. Now we can only imagine what might have happened that day. The following day the phone rang. It was Don's Dad and he was wondering if we had seen Steve. It seemed strange that his car was locked and still at the farm. It seemed strange that no one knew where he was and no one had heard from him. As soon as Don's Dad asked us that question, my immediate response was, "Did you check the barn?" Is there such a thing as a sixth sense? I just knew they would find him there. The following ballad is as close as I can imagine the events as they may have occurred from hearing information from different sources.

Ballad of the Tamed Stallion

The wind blew gusts of sand across a hundred acres of land.
The sun was hot. His lips were parched.
A vacant farm, there he stood just a shell of a man.
He walked across the acres, counting each step.
For Steven knew the outcome of the life he would set.
A loaded gun rested on his shoulder.
He shuffled over the lumpy ground.
He marched along dropping bullets like a zealous soldier.
Steven entered the remnant of an old farming shed.
There he met his destination on a cold damp floor.
There he laid out his deathbed.
He lit one last cigarette, hands shaking, eyes blurred by tears.
Steven was overwhelmed by loneliness and fear.
His pride was broken like a tamed stallion.
Steven wasn't a soldier he had no medallion.
All he had was a life of shattered dreams and faded memories.
His eyes were dimmed by weariness.
All his emotions pulled him deeper into the abyss.
The road ahead seemed far too long.
He felt the load was far too heavy for him to carry on.
He inhaled one last puff of his cigarette.
Blew a breath, to shine a bullet.
Slipped it into the gun and cocked it.
Within the deafening silence of the moment,
Everything around him seemed to subsist.
Angrily he punched the dirt with his fist.
He kicked the ground and stomped like a child.
"To hell with life," He said,
As he squeezed the trigger, then fell over dead.
The farm still remains, but the shed is torn down.
Life's roads twist and turn from town to town.
Like Steven, you might go over a bumpy road or two.

247

Into a town never traveled through.
The road Steven chose is much like that dry, dusty road.
A car riding into the sunset, lost in the dust of his new abode.

When I look back now and after some research, I know that there were some warning signs. If there is one thing that could come out of this chapter, my hope and prayer are that if you know someone suffering with deep depression or suicidal thoughts that they would find refuge, hope and help to overcome their pain. My prayer is that we would learn how to best prevent suicide, by researching this number one cause of death. We might meet people every day who suffer with similar experiences as Steven.

If someone tells you they want to commit suicide, don't panic but do take them seriously. Talk to them and help them by listening to them. If you feel you cannot deal with the situation, call someone with professional experience or knowledge on how to help the distressed person. Never ignore them or hang up on them. Talk to them until they calm down. Pastors, Counselors, suicide help lines, public health units are some areas which may offer you some insight. Also, the Internet is full of information about suicide and prevention. Don't feel you have to deal with this alone. There is help for you and for everyone's future.

If you notice three or more of the following signs in someone you know who is struggling through depression, take them serious and cautiously take the appropriate steps to help this person.

SOME WARNING SIGNS OF SUICIDE

- Abrupt changes in personality.
- Withdrawal or extreme need to tell everyone his or her problem.
- Previous suicide attempt.
- Ending of a relationship.
- Giving away possessions.
- Talk about death or suicide.
- Use of drugs/or alcohol.
- Depression
- Neglect of personal appearance.
- Extreme or extended boredom.
- Hostile behavior.
- Running away from home or school.
- Rebelliousness - reckless behavior.
- Unusual sadness, discouragement and loneliness.
- Unusually long grief reaction.
- Sleeping disturbances.
- Eating disturbances, significant weight changes.
- Obsessive thoughts, discussion on one topic.
- Withdrawal from activities that they love.
- Family disruptions - divorce, trauma, losing loved one.

Field of Dreams
CHAPTER 38

Read (Psalms 31, 40, 42, 46, 57, 77) You may find it helpful if you read these psalms out loud and pray them.

Prayer

O Lord, I need you to help me and give me strength.
Hold me in your arms that I may feel your loving embrace.
Restore within me a Spirit of joy and peace and deliver me
from this place of despair. I need you Lord Jesus to
place me on a solid rock. Take my hand Lord and lead
me out of this depression. Surround me with your love.
Help me Jesus. Please help me I ask thee.

In Jesus powerful name.

39

Roseway
Fiction

❧

Holding on to faith

Roseway sat in a meadow surrounded by endless forest, back dropped by mountains with different shades of reds and greens. The natural beauty of the landscape and the serenity flowing in the air captivated her. She was the portrait of a princess. Her eyes lit up with sparkles of marine green within a velvet brown. Mahogany hair with silky blond highlights danced in the light gentle breeze, completing the innocent softness of her face.

Roseway often went to the meadow of tranquillity to escape reality. Here she would seek peace and refreshment. Roseway would remember a Bible Scripture; Scripture her mother taught her when Roseway was a young child. Whenever she came to the meadow, she would recite the verse. It gave her hope that someday soon her Saviour would hear and answer. For many years Roseway had faithfully said it like a prayer. Something was different about this day. She began to pray: "The Lord is my Shepherd. I shall not want. He makes me to lie down in green pastures."

With an abrupt silence, she stopped after saying a few lines. This time her eyes filled with tears of desperation and frustration, and she cried out to the Lord:

Oh Lord, my mind cannot dance,
My heart cries with sadness.
Where do I go from this place?
Trapped in a desert, so dry,
I long to drink from the water of life.
I long for You to set me free.
Where are you Lord?
Quench this emptiness within my soul.
Now, Oh God.
Allow me to sense Your amazing love.
Oh God!
Set me free.
Rescue me. Rescue me.
Oh Lord, Please rescue me.

Roseway wept, sobbing until she was tired and weak. She sat numb, dazed, as if her mind was drifting some place else. Slowly, her eyes gazed at the sight of a little buttercup. It too was all-alone, lost in a meadow of green. Set apart in the mass of grass, a little buttercup, yellow, bright and flowering like a garden rose. It was flourishing and brilliant bringing vitality to the green meadow. The flower so entranced her as she watched it peak through the ground and reach to the light consummating life. Slowly she reached out her shaking hand to caress its beauty. Tenderly she slipped her fingers around the delicate flower. Her face leaned over the flower trying to breathe a fragrance that would match its beauty. She inhaled the aroma-less scent. Her face took on a blank expression and a stare of disappointment. Roseway glared at the flower sitting helplessly in the palm of her hand. Instantaneously, she closed her hand, smothering the flower.

Vengeful anger gripped her knuckle's white as she ripped the flower from its stem. Slowly, Roseway opened her clutched fingers and looked at the destruction held in the palm of her hand. For only a moment she saw the beauty in the wild flower. Nevertheless, now as she looked at it, she could only see a mirrored image of herself. As she stared, the buttercup slowly fell to the ground.

Feeling like all her hope was gone, Roseway turned and walked away. Shoulders slouched, head facing down she sauntered through the meadow. She was caught in sorrow she had held within her heart for years. Roseway no longer heard the magical music of the singing birds or dancing trees. She only heard the emptiness of her heart that echoed through the chambers of her mind. Walking aimlessly, Roseway came to a stream of swiftly moving water. A group of rocks crowded the stream's edge making it look like an inviting place to rest. Roseway sat hunched over an elevated rock, holding her head in her hands. She was oblivious to the beauty that surrounded her. Then a splash of water lunged at her from the swiftly moving current. She ignored the splash but could not ignore the flopping fish that appeared feet in front of her - or could she? The fish found itself taken from its home, and now desperately trying to get back to the water. Again Roseway sat as if caught in another time and place. Yet her eyes were fixed on the little silver fish flip-flopping, struggling for life. A serene grin came over her face sympathizing for a moment with the little fish. Somehow she could not find it within herself to get off that rock. Something kept her from freeing the fish back to the water of life. Minutes passed by, the silver fish lay in the sand.

The fish's scales were slowly drying, its gills expanding trying to take a breath. Slowing it was dying from lack of water, oxygen and the hot penetrating sun. Suddenly Roseway's stare was interrupted. A gripping wave of water crashed over the shore's edge, pulling the little fish back into the water where it disappeared. Roseway jumped off the rock to rush to the water to see the fish. The misery that minutes ago had kept her company was now gone. Now all she saw was the reflected image of herself, reminded again of the decay slowly eating away any love, she once carried within her heart.

The sun began to set, cooling the night air. Clouds hid the sun like an overbearing lead blanket of dismal grey. Uncomfortable, wet and cold she began to make her way home but where was home? The place she laid her head at night echoed emptiness. Many walls marked the passing years that stood as her foundation reminding her of the hurt and pain. Memories would invade her thoughts, feeding her anxiety. She had so many walls built around her, hemming her in. She felt like she was drowning. "How can I continue," she thought?

Darkness of the night covered the earth yet it felt better than daylight. Perhaps it was because in the dark she could no longer see the walls. She trod the path back to the cabin dragging every step. She listened intently to the crickets and frogs orchestrating a symphony of music. The stars came out one by one adding a pleasant glow to the sky's blackness. Roseway almost found pleasure, as the face on the moon seemed to smile hopefully at her.

Nearing the rustic cabin, the abode of all her sorrow, she slowed her pace. Then glancing ahead a spectacle of light lit the path. As she stretched her vision, she could feel the pounding of her heart increase. With nervous excitement she raced forward to see the blaze.

Heat combed the cool night air as she quickly approached the remnant of the cabin. When she arrived, she saw it crumble to the ground into ashes. Roseway looked intently to find a glimpse of some refuge. A shadow startled Roseway that scurried away into the darkness. She wondered if it could possibly be big Joe? The shadow seemed to fit his image. Joe was big and strong with a heart of coal. The site of the fire-red coals slipped her back into another time and place, into a memory of Big Joe. His big hands, and the smell of smoke and whiskey lingered in her senses. Joe had weatherworn skin, rough and scarred. He was an image firmly imprinted in her mind. His sharp hard voice cut like a pirate's blade. Chills of fear, anger and disgust consumed her. Roseway hoped with all her soul that the shadow was just her feared imagination. She hoped that Joe might be at the bottom of the red-hot coals.

Roseway sat for many hours watching the fire blaze as the walls collapsed into lava hot coals. A sense of peace came over her for the first time in a long time. Feeling like a chained captive set free, a hope of freedom embraced her. The word freedom to Roseway meant no more walls, no more abuse. Overwhelmed by the aspiration she wept tears of joy. Emotions of laughter and tears caused her to sob with such release. She gained ignited hope that she could return to the home she had known as a child. Somewhere out there in the big vast world was her real family from where Joe had stolen her childhood. A place where safety, love, gentleness existed. A place she knew as home. She was anxious to seek out a way to get there, wherever this place might be. One thing she had to do first was to sit quietly until the ashes cooled. Roseway then had one last look at the old cabin of horror. She had to put it to rest.

A couple days had passed. The ashes cooled. She hesitantly walked to where the entrance door once stood. With the still fresh vision of everything in its place, Roseway entered the cabin area. She envisioned the walls that Joe once laced with many pictures of her family.

For so many years these pictures represented her only glimmer of hope. A constant reminder of a family she loved so much. It was for this love Roseway endured and suffered.

In a way she laid down her life so they could live. Joe used these pictures as a threat. He dangled them over her head like candy to a child. Looking through the ashes, Roseway found a half-burned picture. Entranced by the picture she remembered his words, "If ya ever wanna see your family again, you'll do what I tell ya." As she looked at the picture through her teary blurred eyes, she noticed an address on the back. Roseway wiped her eyes with her dirty cuff then clung the picture to her breast. Her only hope was that this address would lead to home. Putting the picture in her pocket, Roseway walked over to where her bed once awaited her.

She grabbed a handful of ashes, took off her shoe then poured the ashes into the shoe. Roseway reached down into the ash heap again and pulled out a brass belt buckle. Imprinted on the front was a charcoal stained "J." She was very familiar with the belt buckle. The only time it left Joe's waist was when he used it on her backside or when he undressed to go to bed. She placed the buckle in the shoe along with the ashes. The sunrise was lighting the horizon. Roseway turned to leave and never return. Just then a raspy voice echoed through her mind. "Don't you dare leave or?" Roseway shook her head to make the voice stop then kept walking. With one shoe on her foot and the other treasure-filled shoe in her hand she continued.

She walked a couple miles feeling more freedom with each passing step. Then she rested under a tall oak tree. While she was sitting beneath the tree, she noticed a little buttercup set apart from any other flowers. Beside it, she dug a little hole and emptied the contents of her shoe. She covered over the hole with soil. Roseway sat and admired the little buttercup, just as she admired the flowering buttercup two days before. This time as she reached down to smell the flower, a tear trickled down her face rolled off her chin, and landed on the delicate flower.

A smile embellished her face as she realized she had

watered the buttercup with her tears. Just as Roseway was about to leave, a gentle breeze began to blow. As she took one last glance at the little grave an acorn fell from the tall oak tree, landing in the hand tilled soil. Roseway turned to continue her journey home.

The sun shone brightly down upon her. The gentle breeze pushed her forward like a loving arm. For the first time she breathed relief, feeling like everything was okay. She felt like her nightmare was finally over. In her heart she believed she would find her way home. A seed of faith had grown. In a meadow of loneliness and desperation God had heard and answered her humble prayer. There was still a journey set before her. She had such peace come over her. Despite all the horrible things of her past, she had a renewed hope to continue. Roseway realized she could rely on God to help her get through any circumstance.

After travelling many miles through the meadow, she came to a roadway. Roseway did not know where the road would take her. Somehow, it didn't really matter because she knew the Lord was leading the way. It was not long before a truck came along. It stopped in front of her. The door opened. The man inside the truck said, "Hello, What is a young girl like you doing way out here? Would you like a ride?" Roseway believed "This is an answer to prayer." "I would appreciate a ride very much." Roseway eagerly entered the truck. The truck driver continued to speak, as they drove down the road, "By the way, my name is Joe! What is your name?"

Let your faith determine the conclusion of this story.

Look for my novel "Roseway."
Coming to book stores 2005

Roseway
CHAPTER 39

1. Roseway uses an example of repetitious prayer. It was the only prayer she had known. For a length of time, the prayer of Psalm 23 sustained her. We see Roseway switches from a prayer she knew, to a prayer she felt. Does God prefer one kind of prayer to another?

2. Many chapters in the bible read like stories. Good guys against the bad guys. Read Psalm 22 and the contrast to Psalm 23. How does David's suffering parallel with the sufferings of Jesus? While Psalm 23 was an encouragement to Roseway for many years, she experienced feelings of loneliness, discouragement and desperation. Roseway cried out fervently to God, much like David in Psalm 22. This shows us that no one person is immune to suffering.

3. Romans 5:3. According to the Bible, what does suffering produce?

4. What was God trying to teach Roseway about herself, with the incident between her and the yellow buttercup?

5. Roseway appreciates God's beautiful creation, but she was so wrought with her own hurts, she became vengeful and angry. In her anxiousness, her faith seemed to wear thin. What are some thoughts and feelings Roseway may have experienced after destroying the buttercup? What do the Psalms reveal about actions Roseway or King David experienced? What was God's reaction?

6. What might Roseway have been feeling, as she watched the little silver fish? How do you think Roseway felt seeing the fish set free? What was God trying to say to Roseway about herself, by using a silver fish?

7. We may have many walls around us. Sometimes we try to ignore or pretend they do not exist. How can we break down these walls, which keep us in bondage? (John 14:15-31, 16:13; 17:6-19) Ephesians 6:10-21; Philippians 4:8

How can you apply what you have recognized in Roseway's life, to help you in your relationship with God and in your daily life?

CONCLUSION

"Letting Go"

❧

A righteous man may have many troubles,
but the Lord delivers him from them all; Psalm 34:19

In life there are many moments when time seems to stand still. We wonder how we will ever get through these times. You may feel like all is lost, as if a downward force pulls you into a tornado and leaves you with no way out.

Many choices brush the horizon. Sometimes it is hard to know which road to travel. You may spend hours or days on your knees in your own garden of Gethsemane, feeling overwhelmed by your circumstance. You may even feel like you would rather die than bear your burden. There is hope for all your woes. Remember you are not alone in that garden. Jesus is in that garden with you. He cried the same prayer and shed the same tears. He walked the road set before him, with strength, determination, enduring all the sufferings you feel and much more. He could have given up the fight, but He did not. Instead He picked up that cross and carried it, up the hill of death. Jesus conquered the task set before him because of His love for us. Jesus conquered death. He is interceding for you today, prodding you to keep going.

For six hours Jesus hung on that cross; six hours time

stood still, as the smell of death lingered in the air. For the ones He loved, Jesus remained on that cross. He finished the good work, which God the Father set before Him. Jesus paid the price for our sins. You can be assured God will finish the good work He began in you. Be like Jesus, endure, be patient and trust in the Father.

With your head held high, take up your cross and carry it. You are not on the cross alone.

Well, it has been a long winding road so far. Many lessons have been learned, some easier than others. Some lessons are still to be learned. From writing my journals or the chapters of my life, I realize the change. I chose the title "When Time Stands Still" because I believe that many of you can relate through your own struggles and times of stillness. My hope and prayer are that you will receive comfort, hope and love to get you through the days ahead. The main truth I pray you hear and receive is that Jesus can be right beside you, through any circumstance. Whatever we strive to find in life, we can find in Him.

The change takes place when we learn to submit to God with all our hearts and let go of our will and walk in His perfect will. That is when we truly find Him. In reality we are the ones lost and He not only knows exactly where we are, but He saves us from our selves. This has been a tough lesson to grasp for myself. When I stop fighting God's will, and give the battle of self to Jesus, life makes much more sense. It is a continual process of giving everything over to God. Let go of our fears, pain, questions or whatever we struggle with because they will only hinder our relationship and growth with God and others.

I believe Dorothy from the wizard of oz said it best: "We don't have to look any further than our own back yard." Jesus is waiting at your door to be invited in. We all have moments in our lives when time seems to stands still. We can also have that inner peace knowing everything will work out fine. When time stands still God is closer than ever. It is then that we draw closer to Him. In drawing closer and crying out to Him, our tears mix with His. God's love for us is like no other love you will ever find, anywhere else.

It is comforting to know that we have an eternal Father and Friend, who cares enough to discipline us and show us the path to take. He rubs hard sometimes, but in the end we will be clean and spotless. The process is like a piece of coal being polished. When He is finished polishing us, we are more like beautiful diamonds. This preparation is for the eternal day, in a new heaven and a new earth. Where we will live with Him in that place where TIME STANDS STILL for eternity.

You can begin your new life in Jesus Christ today.

My Decision:
To Receive Christ Jesus as My Saviour

Name

Date

I confess to You God that I am a sinner, and ask you Jesus to forgive my sins. I ask you to take total control of my life by becoming my Lord and personal Saviour. I ask you to walk with me always and lead me through all the days of my life. I believe that you Jesus are the Christ and that you died for my sins on the cross and that you were raised from the dead for my justification. I do now receive you and confess You Jesus as my personal Saviour. Thank you to God, Father, Son, and Holy Spirit, in the name of Jesus Christ I pray. Amen!

Printed in the United States
26370LVS00003BA/58-255

9 781594 677274